I0135312

WANDERING IN GREECE
ATHENS, ISLANDS AND ANTIQUITIES

Other Wanderland Writers Anthologies

WANDERING IN GREECE
ATHENS, ISLANDS AND ANTIQUITIES

Edited by
Linda Watanabe McFerrin and
Joanna Biggar

Wanderland Writers
Oakland, California

Copyright © 2020 Wanderland Writers. All rights reserved.
No part of this publication may be reproduced, distributed, or transmitted in
any form or by any means, including photocopying, recording, or other
electronic or mechanical methods, without the prior written permission of the
publisher, except in the case of brief quotations embodied in critical reviews
and certain other noncommercial uses permitted by copyright law.

For permission to print essays in this volume, grateful acknowledgement is
made to the holders of copyright named on pages 175–183.

The poem beginning on page 1 is an extract from "The Blue Museum,"
in *The Blue Museum: Poems*, Sisyphus Press, 2004.

The poem beginning on page 155 was previously published in 2006 in
Venturing in Southern Greece: The Vatika Odysseys.

Photographs:
Front cover © Laurie McAndish King
Back cover portrait © Lowry McFerrin
Pages 70, 182 © Joanna Biggar
Pages 18, 20 © Connie Burke
Page xx © Phil Cousineau
Pages 146, 166 © Barbara J. Euser
Page 106 © Annelize Goedbloed
Page 50 © Donna Hemmila
Pages vi, 22, 42, 66, 86, 96, 120, 128, 154, 174 © Laurie McAndish King
Pages 58, 136 © Lowry McFerrin
Page 32 © Gayle McGill
Page 158 © MJ Pramik
Page 112 © Heather Tomlinson
Page 183 © Alison Wright

Pages 4, 78, 100, 138: public domain
Page 14 © Sting, CC BY-SA 2.5, Wikimedia Commons

Cover design, interior design and map by Jim Shubin,
www.bookalchemist.net

CATALOGING DATA:
Wandering in Greece: Athens, Islands and Antiquities
Edited by Linda Watanabe McFerrin and Joanna Biggar

ISBN: 978-1-7348251-8-3
First printing 2020
Printed in the United States of America

For Nanos Valaoritis (1921–2019)

beloved poet, novelist, playwright, translator, and scholar

Special thanks to Connie Leones Burke, a wonderful friend to Wanderland Writers, whose generosity, hard work and insider's knowledge did so much to make this adventure possible.

Welcome to Greece

CONTENTS

GREECE

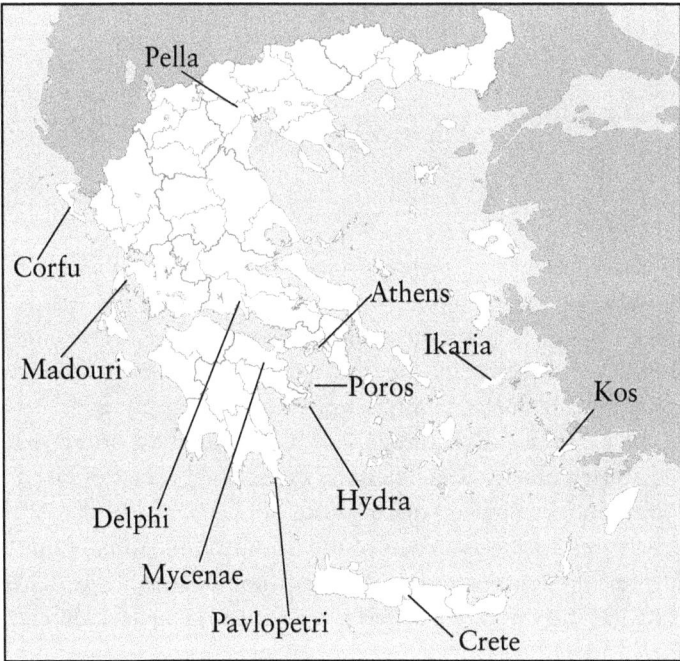

INTRODUCTION

"Tell me, O muse, of travellers far and wide."
—*Homer*

And so we return to Greece ... once again we set out with a band of writers—and yet alone—to lose ourselves amid the islands, on the rocky shores, upon those wine-dark seas of legend and lore. We follow, of course, in the footsteps of heroes, philosophers, romantics, explorers, painters, writers and, some say, gods.

We begin our adventure in Athens, in the midst of the village-like warren of narrow cobblestone streets and businesses called the Plaka, and in Piraeus, the bustling port city within the Athens urban area on the east coast of the Saronic Gulf. Some want, like Daphne du Maurier, to "see the Parthenon by moonlight." Others revel in location so thick with myth that, as Percy Jackson creator Rick Riordan declared, "You can't swing a cat ... without hitting one of Zeus's girlfriends."

From this historically and culturally rich Attic center, our roving writers spread out to explore the islands, the villages, the highways and byways of ancient and modern Greece in search of Alexander, of oracles, of gods, of goddesses, of mystery, of modernization, of wine and food and gardens, of widening awareness and profound realization.

"We are all Greeks. Our laws, our literature, our religion, our arts have their root in Greece," wrote an effusive Percy Bysshe Shelley in ferociously romantic times.

Well, we may not actually be Greek, but we do feel this culture's call, and we think you will see in these stories and poems that the travelers who come to Greece as seekers will find, as Lawrence Durrell once wrote, *themselves*—and generally so much more—on the journey.

—Linda Watanabe McFerrin and Joanna Biggar
Oakland, California

FOREWORD

"Enter the dark crystal if you dare
And gaze on Greece."
—*Lawrence Durrell*

In 1766, the English antiquarian Richard Chandler was sent by the Society of Dilettanti on an archaeological expedition to search for antiquities in Greece and Ionia. After venturing around Athens, where he purchased several fragments of sculpture that had fallen from the tumbledown Parthenon, Chandler headed toward Arcadia, on the Peloponnese peninsula, in search of the long-lost site of Ancient Olympia.

As the story goes, when Chandler arrived in the serenely beautiful valley, at the point where the Alpheios River meets the Kladeos, he paused to read from his leather-bound copy of *Descriptions of Greece* by the second century traveler and geographer Pausanias. Arguably the first travel writer in history, and one of the original ruin-haunters, Pausanius described in astonishing detail the religious art and architectural marvels of the seventy temples and treasuries and athletic facilities within the Sanctuary of Zeus. Despite the precise descriptions of the site, Chandler saw nothing resembling ancient temples or training grounds. Nothing other than oak woods and olive groves, goat herds and shepherds.

Suddenly, Chandler later recalled, a single ray of scintillating Greek sunlight glinted off a chunk of marble sticking out of the riverbank that had been exposed by recent floodwaters. His heart raced as he dug with his bare hands until he recognized a carved Doric capital, then the flutes of a colossal column.

By dint of chance, perhaps the nod of the gods, Chandler found himself standing atop the ruins of the Temple of Zeus, one of the Seven Wonders of the Ancient World, the temenos at the heart of the sanctuary. Looking up, he tried to imagine the rest of the massive complex where pilgrims came from all over the Mediterranean to worship the Thunder Lord and to enjoy the Great Games, which were held alongside competitions in drama, oratory, dancing and drinking, every four years without cessation for over fifteen centuries. But the entire site was now buried underneath twenty-six feet of silt and rubble, the result of pillage, earthquakes, tsunamis and the depredations of the Roman emperor Theodosius who razed the site in 396 CE, as part of his parched earth program to destroy any memory of so-called pagan Greece.

And so Ancient Olympia vanished, forgotten for fifteen centuries, until Chandler's chance discovery and the first official excavations and preservation, which began in 1829 and lasted until 1996.

Those efforts at Olympia and at sites all around the ancient world are reminders that memory itself is a sacred and tenuous thing. Our very souls depend on it. The ancient Greeks said as much by personifying it as the goddess Mnemosyne, who was, not coincidentally, the mother of the Nine Muses. In the spirited picture language of mythology this means that inspiration and memory are inextricably connected; we can't have one without the other.

To me, this connection helps explain the thrill of recognition for those who followed in the footsteps of Chandler and his fellow dilettanti, those peripatetic poets, artists, architects, designers and philosophers who embarked upon the Grand Tour to Italy and Greece. As the poet Percy Shelley wrote in what could be an epigraph for this marvel-filled anthology, "We are all Greeks. Our laws, our literature, our religion, our arts have their root in Greece." By tracking down the roots of Western Civilization, those intrepid travelers not only helped reinvigorate their own lives through their encounters with history and the breathtaking beauty of the Greek landscape, they eventually ignited the bittersweet phenomenon of mass tourism.

I deeply identify with this belief because I grew up "on the knee of Homer," reading the classics with my father. But as deeply as I felt the thrill of reading about the polyfabulous world of Odysseus, Penelope, Aphrodite and Hermes, I needed to experience the *frisson*, the shiver-up-the-spine experience, of seeing Greece for myself.

On my very first night in Athens, in the tumultuous spring of 1975, there were tanks in the streets and tear gas in the air, so I escaped the madness by strolling up to the then unguarded Acropolis and camped out *inside* the Parthenon, gazing up at the full moon in all its melancholic splendor, sipping wine from my bota bag, and reading from my father's copy of the *Iliad*.

In some mysterious way, I have been trying to recapture the essence of that experience ever since, which to me is the essence of travel, an insight into the infinite moment, what Henry Miller described as "the stillness of the world" at Epidaurus, and Dame

Rose Macaulay called "the broken beauty" of the ancient ruins of Bassae and Ephesus.

For me, this is where the hope of the avid traveler and the aspiration of the ardent reader are aligned. Both are motivated by the longing for a glimpse of the *deeply real*, the underglimmer of truth that lies below the spuriousness of commercial travel.

This marvelous new anthology scratches both existential itches. The very title, *Wandering in Greece*, evokes a Greek aphorism, "To philosophize is to wander." In turn, the saying echoes one of my favorite theories about the mysterious source of its Golden Age, which is the unbounded curiosity of early Greek travelers venturing to the very edge of the known world.

As I riffled the pages that comprise the wide-ranging entries of this collection, I often thought of Richard Chandler and his serendipitous encounter with Taphos, the light, the tremulous, quivering light at Olympia and all over the miracle that is the Mediterranean world. What surges forth in these pages is more than historical information. Again and again, what illuminates these stories is what Albert Camus remarked in his essay on Helen of Troy, "The Greeks died for beauty."

Not the sentimental variety, but the numinous quality. The beauty that is forged on the anvil of tragedy and, in the case of Greece, centuries of foreign occupation, civil war, and economic calamity. The transcendent beauty suggested by the French novelist Stendahl when he wrote, "Beauty is the promise of happiness."

This is the intoxicating lure of the traveler's tale, the travel poster, the song about romantic destinations, not the guarantee but the *possibility* of a moment of happiness, and even, if the gods are smiling upon our woebegone souls, joy.

Finally, I believe this book speaks to our own historical moment. In the spirit of Mark Twain, who famously wrote that "Travel is fatal to prejudice, bigotry, and narrow-mindedness," these stories embody the sacred Greek code of *xenia*, hospitality, kindness to strangers and travelers. For some unfathomable reason, the noble concept was transmogrified into *xenophobia*, the fear or disdain of others, while too often forgetting its original sense of *xenophilia*, the welcoming of strangers, as well as an affection for unknown places and people.

Wandering in Greece not only takes us back to where we began, it helps use recognize ourselves in others.

—*Phil Cousineau*
San Francisco 2020

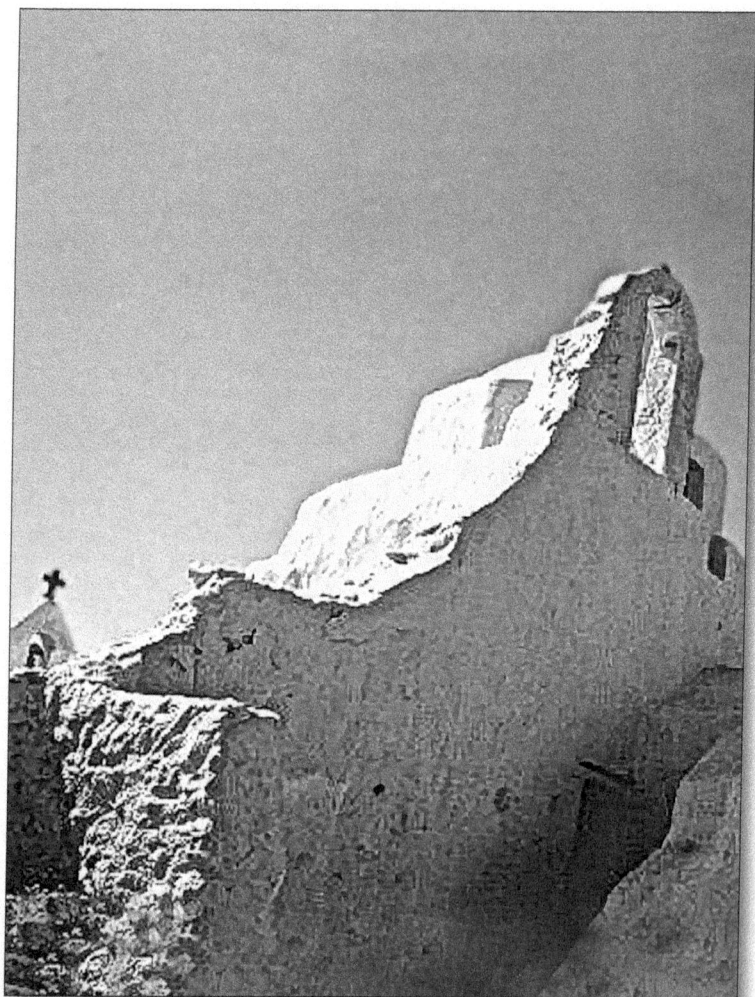

The White Chapel, Mykonos

THE BLUE MUSEUM

Phil Cousineau

"The fisherman of Mithyrum, having cast their nets into the
sea, drew them in and discovered a head carved from
the wood of an olive tree."
—*Pausanius, second century*

1.
There on the briny shores of Naxos,
on the edge of the ultramarine sea,
where the scorching sun blisters old stones,
and makes the lemony light tremble,
I sit on a gently swaying, creaking wooden pier
watching an aged fisherman with salt-swollen hands
empty gleaming nets of flailing fish.
Calmly, he catches them one by one in mid-air
as they try to defy gravity and evade their fate,
the single blow from the old wooden mallet
wielded by his softly singing, black-shawled wife.
There where the island sky hurries into heavenly blue
and the whitewashed windmills creak and groan,

The fisherman sets the fish down on the pier
as gently as one of the local Greek Orthodox priests
lays communion wafers on the tongues of the faithful.
Mumbling like an old soothsayer, he speaks to each of them
In the dark-keeled words of his ancestors,
grateful for the bounty.

2.
His name is Manoles and his face is crimped
with wrinkles, hard-earned lifelines
revealing the map of his secret knowledge
about the cobalt blue world that surrounds him.
He smiles like a pelican with a good haul in his beak,
squats down on the pier with a fistful of dripping,
multi-colored net. Methodically,
he mends the severed threads
while naming the different kinds of fish he caught
during the long night on the spuming sea,
ancient Greek nouns that sound as exotic and remote as
Homer's catalogue of ships that set sail for Troy.
Without looking up from his task, Manoles says
that on certain mornings, with the mist
"as gray as the eyes of the goddess Athena,"
he sometimes finds stranger things than fish tangled in his nets.
"Old coins. Old urns. Old statues."
His voice drops weightlessly,
then floats on the salty air
like the corks he fastens to his nets.

"The sea, she is full of treasures from the ships
of our father's father's fathers
that sank long ago—"
Suddenly, he stops, frustrated by his fractured English,
then speaks with his rope-burned hands, shaping them
into a ship whose prow dips in and out of the glittering waves.
Smiling now like an old sea lion, he adds,
"Statues, beautiful bronze statues,
statues we find at the bottom of the sea.
That is why we call her
the blue museum."

Alexander the Great mosaic, ca. 100 BCE

Waiting for Alexander

Anne Sigmon

"It is delightful to live a life of valour and to die leaving
behind immortal glory."
— *Alexander the Great*, quoted by Arrian in
The Anabasis of Alexander

Some women receive pearls on their wedding day. My husband,
Jack, gave me a twenty-three-hundred-year-old coin, a tetradrachm
of Alexander the Great set in a gold necklace. As I floated down the
candlelit aisle, the young king hung around my neck in a profile of
unlimited promise.

That coin from my new husband rekindled my interest in
Alexander. In 356 BCE, at only twenty years old, he was crowned
king of Macedon, a kingdom on the periphery of ancient Greece.
Although he reigned for barely twelve years, he is still regarded as
one of history's finest military minds.

As Jack and I traveled over the ensuing years, we sought out sites
and relics connected to Alexander from Turkey to Persia, Lebanon
and Syria. Now, more than two decades after I received my
necklace, we were in Greek Macedonia exploring Alexander's roots
at his birthplace in Pella, the capital of ancient Macedon. It felt like
a promise coming full circle.

But it was not what I expected.

On a sere plain that once overlooked an outlet to the Aegean Sea, ancient Pella is today reduced to marble foundations outlined in dry grass. Only a few columns stand to recall its glory days.

As I walked through Pella's deserted ruins, I imagined the capital as it had been in the age leading up to Alexander. One of the most impressive precincts of the ancient world, Pella was a celebrated capital of lustrous stone houses with columned porticoes, rich paintings, vibrant pebble mosaic floors, bustling shops, and a renowned library. In those days, the music of lyres mingled with the scent of lilac and orange blossoms. Painters and poets strolled the marble colonnades and lush gardens.

The story of Alexander's astonishing conquest really begins here, with his titanic father, who revolutionized ancient warfare. King Philip II seized the Macedonian crown in 359 BCE. Philip, stocky and tough, declared the mythical hero Hercules as an ancestor. When he ascended the throne, he faced a maelstrom of foreign threats and rival pretenders to his kingship. Philip was a shrewd, quick-tempered, hard-drinking man who was one of the greatest military commanders of the ancient world. It was Philip's ambition to unite Macedonia and the ever-tumultuous Greek City States and, ultimately, to move against their ancient common enemy, the Persians.

Alexander's mother, Olympias, was a princess of the western Balkan kingdom of Epirus. She was red-haired, fiery, proud and deeply religious. As mother to the heir to the throne, she reigned as queen. Olympias was a fervent devotee of the snake-handling cult of the Dionysian mysteries. According to Alexander biographer Mary Renault, Olympias was "turbulent, uncanny, wild as a Thracian *maenad*, able, if she was crossed, to put the evil eye on you."

Some ancient gossips whispered that Philip's ardor for Olympias cooled when he found snakes writhing in her bed. According to Renault, "The violent fracture of their relations must have happened in Alexander's early childhood .... By the time he was in his teens, they were not merely estranged but open enemies." What effect the trauma of a toxic childhood had on Alexander we can only guess. We know that he was a serious child who, against all reason, never seemed afraid.

The opulent throne room at Pella was Alexander's playground. He was curious, more like a learned schoolboy than a scholar. His childhood tutor was Leonidas, Olympias's uncle, a hard disciplinarian who admired the austere customs of Sparta. Under his tutelage, Alexander was taught to eschew princely luxury; he slept on the hard stone floors and often went without a cloak in frigid weather.

Alexander was, even as a boy, a quick, light-footed hunter. He was short—about 5'7" as an adult—but handsome, with a high-bridged nose and a pale complexion that flushed red with anger or exertion. At twelve or thirteen years old, he famously tamed the furiously wild horse named Bucephalus—Oxhead.

From childhood, Alexander had a longing to excel. He was, Plutarch wrote, steeped with *philotimia*, the love of honor. According to historians, Alexander grew up with an almost religious faith in friendship. He developed a close circle of friends—boys, most of them older, who played together at the palace, studied together, trained together, fought together, and continued to serve as Alexander's close advisors for the rest of his life. They included the famous general Ptolemy and Hephaestion, Alexander's dearest and closest friend.

When Alexander was thirteen, in 343 BCE, Philip invited the esteemed philosopher Aristotle to be his son's tutor. Aristotle established a school for Alexander and his friends near a wooded sanctuary dedicated to water nymphs by the town of Mieza about twenty miles from Pella.

Mieza has been a sacred place for thousands of years. Jack and I drove there, parked and walked across a wooden bridge toward the meadow where Aristotle's school once stood. In this cool, still-numinous space, dappled sunlight played on the ivy, ferns and vines. What I noticed most was the silence, as though even nature bowed in prayer. In the meadow, rimmed by a cavernous twenty-foot rock face with still-visible classrooms carved into the tufa, we saw slashes and post holes that once held the roof and a colonnade. I sat on the rim of an old well, imagining Aristotle, pacing up and down, igniting Alexander's passions—for exploration, for botany, zoology, medicine, history and the art of war.

Aristotle's highest charge to Alexander the Great was this: "Be what you wish to seem." It was a charge he took to heart for the rest of his life. At just sixteen years old, he left Aristotle's school and returned to Pella to serve as regent while his father battled the Greek City States. I imagine Alexander's deep-set gray-blue eyes unflinching as he peered up at the taller, older men. What internal steel made him seem, even then, indomitable?

Soon, Alexander left the court to join his father's cavalry in a series of battles that honed his leadership skills, culminating with the seminal Battle of Chaeronea in August 338 BCE. There on the plain of ancient Boeotia in Central Greece, Philip faced a coalition of Greek City States led by Thebes and Athens.

On a scorching June afternoon, Jack and I drove through the country near the modern town of Chaeronea looking for the battle site. Our first clue was the cypress trees, which still mark important gravesites throughout Greece. On the afternoon of our visit, the air seemed to burn with the brand of history.

With only cicadas for company, my husband and I struggled to fathom the bloody horrors of that day when the world first glimpsed Alexander's greatness—the violence and pandemonium of the battle where Alexander's unit faced the vaunted Sacred Band, a three-hundred-strong elite force of the Theban army. Undefeated in forty years of existence, the Band was destroyed that day by Alexander's cavalry in one of his first outings as a commander. He was eighteen years old.

Impressed with the Sacred Band's courage, Philip allowed a monument—a statue of a lion—to be erected on the site to commemorate their sacrifice. Incredibly, the Lion of Chaeronea still survives today, a nearly twenty-foot-tall grieving beast that sits in a depression of grass on top of an equally tall modern plinth. The beast dwarfs all who stand beside it, a dramatic reminder not only of the Thebans' sacrifice but also of Alexander's glorious victory and a decisive moment in world history.

After the battle of Chaeronea, Philip was master of the Greek peninsula. Over the next two years, with Alexander's help, he consolidated his victory and began planning an invasion of Persia—the climax of two hundred years of Greek-Persian enmity.

But Philip's court was riven by rivalry and intrigue. Two years after Chaeronea, in 336 BCE, long-seated rancor and jealousy exploded in shocking regicide: Philip was assassinated by one of his bodyguards, brutally stabbed in full view at a public festival. The cause appeared to be a personal feud. But from ancient times to modern, gossips (and some historians, including Plutarch) have whispered that Olympias—though never implicated directly—surely stoked the acrimony that drove the murder plot.

After Philip's death, Alexander secured his power over the Greeks and led his army to complete his father's long-dreamed conquest of Persia. In thirteen years of unprecedented generalship, Alexander coalesced the notoriously balky Greeks, overthrew the mighty Persians, and built a progressive and, for its day, tolerant empire that blanketed the known world from Greece to India. But after he plowed into India in 326 BCE, his exhausted army would go no farther. According to Plutarch, "When Alexander saw the breadth of his domain, he wept for there were no more worlds to conquer."

Alexander's will to explore was undiminished, but his health—and some say his judgment—was sapped by the after-effects of hard drinking, a series of grievous battle injuries and the shocking death of Hephaestion. Eight months after Hephaestion's death—in June 323 BCE—Alexander died in Babylon of a sudden illness, probably typhoid fever. He was, at thirty-two years old, arguably the greatest military commander the world had ever seen.

Other than his military victories, what made Alexander great?

"Alexander could transmit imagination as others could transmit lust," Aristotle once said.

According to biographer Mary Renault, "his insistence on sharing every danger to which he exposed his men was almost an obsession. Alexander was entirely trusted, constantly and deeply loved."

I was struck by another trait: Alexander tried to govern more justly than his father and to treat his household with more respect. Even in brutal times, "his most striking peculiarity was his refusal to exploit defenseless victims," Renault wrote. Alexander envisioned an integrated society. He adopted Persian customs and resisted enslaving those he conquered—sometimes to the chagrin of followers who didn't understand his vision.

Alexander also introduced the concept of interconnectedness. During his lifetime, Greek thought and culture began to reshape the ideas and beliefs of conquered populations, a process that continued long after he died. History calls it Hellenization. This intermingling of ideas was spread in part through a web of trade connections in Europe, the Middle East and Asia formed during Alexander's reign. We call it globalization today. And there are many modern oppo-nents just as there were in Alexander's time. Today, as then, people rail at change.

As I thought about this, I looked at the reminders of Alexander cluttered around my desk. I picked up my favorite picture of him—a marble head sculpted from life by the famed artist Leochares. I saw the trademark tousled hair, the steely assurance in his steady gaze. But somewhere around the mouth I sensed compassion, a tenderness that I pictured as the other side of Alexander—perhaps the true root of his greatness.

Putting the photo aside, I lifted my Alexander necklace from its case. As I studied his young face, I surprised myself when I started to cry.

Was I weeping for lost years? For a path grown narrow and fleeting since I first wore this beautiful coin on my wedding day? Maybe. But as I brushed the tears aside, I realized I was really grieving for what I think Alexander represented—the imperfect but sincere reach for a more just and inclusive world.

My lifetime has been blessed with a number of leaders who, like Alexander, reached for the good, inspiring us all to believe in a world enriched rather than diminished by difference. Things weren't perfect, I knew. But, until recently, I had faith that society was improving over time. That day, I cried in frustration at how far we've regressed. Today, I cringe at leaders—not just in the United States where I live but in many parts of the world—who stoke fear and provoke hatred by embracing nativism, separatism, the xenophobia of "other-ism."

Some days I despair. But I am by nature an optimist. So I put on my wedding necklace to wear it for a while, a talisman for reassurance that the day will come—surely not so far off—when a modern-day Alexander will burst forth to lead us toward our better selves.

Herm of Alexander the Great

THREE HERMS
Greek, 4th Century BCE

Linda Watanabe McFerrin

The noseless
head of Alexander
surmounts this column
like some trophy on
a pike,
accompanied
by the head of a
companion,
perhaps Hephaiston,
his beloved friend.
We know his features
from one inscribed
relief
in Thessalonika,
in which Hephaiston,
standing quietly,
flanks the

mobile thirty-three year old
who conquered half
the world.
The third head
in this triplet is
a lady whose coiffure
is large and
melon-shaped;
her nose and mouth are lost
in speechless adoration,
soft,
her features and her eyes
the sorrowful companions
to these men.

Our attention is called
to the pierced lobes of her ears.

Water jar with fountain scene
Attic, ca. 510-500 BCE

Vase Painting I

Connie Burke

Five women in an ancient world, whisper
Of fallen heroes while filling their jars
With requiem waters whose apertures
Pour libations over perished souls afar.

Hydriai rest heavily on tules
Cushioned on their heads, a sad reminder
Of a warrior culture, Achilles
Leonidas, Jason, Alexander.

Scenes of warriors fighting for glory,
Their lust for wars untamable like flies.
Dories and hoplans telling their story
Of grief, fear and the authorship of lies.

Albeit Athens or Afghanistan,
Libation waters cease to cleanse their hands.

Bowl for mixing wine and water with masks of Dionysos
and a satyr, Attic, ca. 520-510 BCE

VASE PAINTING II

Connie Burke

Befitting the moment, Dionysos,
God of wine, festivities and frenzy,
Whose evil-expelling eyes, glare at us,
Sanctioning our every sip with envy.

With an inch of day left, drums softly beat,
Echoing rhythms of a Bacchic rite.
We sway, like supple branches in retreat,
Freeing the beast within, a woman's plight.

Filling our thirsty cups we drink and dance
Like Lowell's naked fauns too glad for shame.
Cleansing and cathartic, wholly entranced,
We drop our Master's mask and feed our flames.

Celebrating rituals of the vine,
We praise Silenus by drinking more wine.

A wine-pouring robot at the Museum of
Ancient Greek Technology

Back to the Future

Tom Harrell

Athenians crowd the high Acropolis, the temples filled with the sounds and smells of fear. The people cry out to their patron goddess Athena for protection from what is coming.

Below, robots are on the march. Women created from bronze and paint to serve wine lead the way; their eyes alive. Mechanical birds, made merely to amuse, fly ahead. Pigeons, once powered by steam, now float on the winds of freedom. Or is it revenge? Behind, weapons of war draw ever closer, propelled as if by magic by ingenious gears and valves and pulleys: steam-powered cannons and flame throwers, siege towers ten stories high and giant claws built to capture entire ships, heat rays from the captured sun. An army of mechanical slaves has risen, and they will not be content with mere freedom.

That fanciful day, of course, occurred only in my imagination as I left the Museum of Ancient Greek Technology in Athens. Which I found, by the way, using old-fashioned intuition and a paper map, my modern American technology showpiece—the iPhone—refusing to cooperate without a WiFi connection.

The Museum packs an amazing amount of information, and reconstructed models of *ancient* technology, into a renovated townhouse near Syntagma Square. Around me, adults and children alike delighted in the working models and marveled—even in the age of *Siri* and *Alexa*—at the ancient automatic temple doors, seeming to open by divine will; the coin-operated vending machines; the hydraulic alarm clock attributed to Plato (perhaps spurred to invention by tardy students); and, of course, the life-size copy of the robot servant, a woman designed to serve wine to guests and animated by hidden pulleys and siphons.

Greece is famous for its remarkable temples and ruins, enduring reminders of its ancient glory. And lasting longer than even stone and marble are the ancient Greeks' advances in philosophy, art, mathematics, geometry, astronomy and engineering. But the applications of that ancient genius, the technology that emerged from brilliant minds to assist or merely to amuse, is less well known. For many, classical Greece is little more than Troy and ruined temples and distant, dusty philosophy. Few imagine ancient Greece as a Silicon Valley in sandals, a hotbed of invention and science—albeit developed over several hundred years.

What, I wondered, could we learn from the ancient Greeks? Not from their technology, impressive as it was, which we have copied and surpassed. As we confront existential questions of the role of technology in society, as our fears multiply, fears of artificial intelligence and big data and facial recognition and the possible misuse of technologies so esoteric as to seem like magic—and yes, of a robot rebellion—what can we learn from a technological revolution over two thousand years old?

From the time of the rediscovery of classical learning—the Renaissance—Western society has been plagued by tension between science and religion, often viewed as inherently incompatible. Such was not the case in ancient Greece. The Greeks worshipped a complex and shifting panoply of gods, goddesses, and lesser deities. While the gods and goddesses lived in splendor high on Mt. Olympus, they often squabbled amongst themselves, interfered in human affairs, and were remarkably accessible.

For the Greeks, technology was not something that challenged the divinity of the gods and goddesses, but was, rather, a gift from and natural part of the relationship between the Greeks and those they worshipped. Hephaestus—a son of Zeus and the god of craft, blacksmithing, and "technology"—was revered on Mt. Olympus for his skills and was famous among the Greeks for his many clever inventions, including Talos, the "cyborg" giant made to protect Crete until undone by Jason and the Argonauts and Medea; the impenetrable armor of Achilles; and twenty "walking tripods" with golden wheels and minds of their own that awed even the gods.

The close connection between Mt. Olympus and invention seems to have removed any divine objection to advances in technology. And the fertile trade routes between Greek City States and their successful colonies in the Aegean, the Turkish coast, Italy, Sicily, and later Alexandria with its incomparable library, incubated, stimulated, and disseminated knowledge throughout the Greek world. The ancient Greek would not have been surprised to see and use technology, including "automata," or human-like "machines." As early as the fifth century BCE, the poet Pindar, in an ode to the Panhellenic games, described the island of Rhodes matter-of-factly:

> The animated figures stand
> Adorning every public street
> And seem to breathe in stone, or
> Move their marble feet.

The fertile marriage of advancing science, including pneumatics and hydraulics; mathematics and metallurgy; engineering; and meticulous craft manufacture, produced a number of startling inventions. Most had practical uses, such as the odometer and twin-piston pump. Many were driven by the needs of warfare, as is sometimes the case today, such as the repeating catapult and Archimedes' ideas of a parabolic "heat ray" and steam cannon—a design later refined by Leonardo da Vinci.

Some were for entertainment and were a marvel to behold: the first "moving pictures" that combined sound, movement, and animation to create ancient cinema—including a "movie" about the Trojan War; or programmable puppet shows staged with animatronic figures that unfolded in a precise and life-like choreography of "scenes" by way of hidden strings and pulleys.

Still other technologies were of limited utility, but ingenious nonetheless: the coin-operated vending machine that dispensed holy water; singing mechanical birds; a flying pigeon propelled by jet propulsion; and the realistic mechanical servant built to serve wine whenever a cup was placed in her hand.

So common was the use of technology that by 322 BCE Aristotle could imagine a future dependent on technology—and independent of servitude.

In his *Politics*, Aristotle speculated, "There is only one condition in which we can imagine managers not needing subordinates and masters not needing slaves. This condition would be that each instrument could do its own work, at the word of command or by intelligent anticipation..." In a world where labor was always in shortage and slavery widespread, such a future must have seemed ideal indeed.

As the power, if not the influence, of Greece waned and that of Rome rose, the apotheosis of ancient Greek technology seems to have been reached with the first "analog computer," the famous Antikythera Mechanism. The Antikythera Mechanism is a machine about the size of a small suitcase, and indeed appears to have been built to aid navigation as well as to calculate simultaneously the positions of the sun and moon; the orbits of the five planets then known to the Greeks (Mercury, Venus, Mars, Jupiter, and Saturn); eclipses; several different calendar cycles common in the Greek world, including the Egyptian 365-day year; and the cycles of the four Panhellenic games: Pythian, Nemean, Isthmian, and of course Olympic.

The Antikythera Mechanism was found in 1900 among the sunken ruins of a Roman cargo ship off the Greek island of Antikythera. After two thousand years under the sea, the Mechanism was little more than a lump of oxidized bronze. Treated as a curiosity at first, over the subsequent decades advances in science have allowed us to discover ever more of how it worked, though there is still vigorous debate over its age, origin, and purposes.

Though some parts are missing, the Antikythera Mechanism was made of at least thirty bronze gears and thirty-seven gear wheels operated by a drive train. Ingeniously interconnected, the gear wheels rotated in unison when cranked to align the multiple functions. The original Mechanism and several replicas made since—no two identical, as scientists disagree over its precise design—now rest at the National Archeological Museum in Athens. The complexity and craftsmanship—the tiny bronze gears were cut by hand—are stunning. The replicas—their shining brass guts reminiscent of Escher or Rube Goldberg at any angle—mesmerize.

It is little wonder that the Antikythera Mechanism was found aboard a sunken Roman ship, probably en route from Rhodes to Rome. It was possibly on its way to a triumphal parade to be staged for Julius Caesar, a metaphorical elephant of science to awe the masses. What struck me immediately upon seeing the replicas of the Mechanism was my family connection, not to its history or grandiose purposes, but to its exquisite craftsmanship. My grandfather was a watch repairman in Georgia, and I inherited from him his tools of the trade, if not his skill and patience.

On a far smaller scale, a traditional watch is really a piece of technology akin to the Antikythera Mechanism: a miniature machine made of multiple, artfully balanced gears, a beautiful thing, able to keep precise time, calculate the day and date, and even track the phases of the moon. I could imagine his wonder, his respect, for the craftsmen of ancient Greece. The very word "technology" derives from the Greek word *techne*, meaning craft skill. Two thousand years may have passed between the technologists behind the Antikythera Mechanism and my grandfather's humble jewelry shop, but on that day, as a modern man standing in awe as much as any Roman would have upon witnessing such genius, time seemed a fleeting thing.

That timeless connection, more than any museum or temple or statue, left me humbled by the ancient Greeks, in my heart as well as my mind. Alas, I must admit that, like my iPhone when separated from WiFi, the Antikythera Mechanism was far from perfect. Despite the brilliance of its predictive models, including the elliptical orbit of the moon, the Mechanism depended on faulty Greek assumptions about astronomy. As we say today, junk in, junk out. Moreover, the mechanism was bound to grow less accurate with time. Meticulous as the craftsmanship was, the handmade bronze gears were bound to wear and loosen. Undoubtedly, there were craftsmen, men like my grandfather, with the tools and knowledge to fix this marvel. But if so, they are lost to history, their knowledge slowly washed away as surely as the Mechanism itself.

Maybe, I thought, *it was a blessing in disguise to sink in its prime, patiently waiting to amaze, before age and error tarnished its beauty.*

Still, two thousand years later it is hard to nitpick the knowledge and skills of the ancient Greeks, especially when it turns out that, unbeknownst to me and my fellow writers armed with computers and above all Google, there are TWO museums of ancient technology in Athens. Who knew ancient technology was so popular? I discovered this when comparing notes with a fellow writer in the group, who mentioned she had also visited the museum. It soon became apparent either we inhabited parallel universes or there were "parallel" museums.

The latter seemed more likely and, indeed, it turns out Athens hosts two museums of ancient Greek technology. Determined to investigate, I set out one afternoon to find the other museum. Venturing confidently, if foolishly, off the road more traveled (and better marked), I made a few wrong turns below the Hill of Nymphs, whose laughter I could almost hear. Had they summoned the unseasonable drizzle?

I prayed to whatever gods or goddesses remained in residence near the Acropolis for direction, and I tell you true, I received a messenger just as my weary legs demanded I give up and slink back to the main road. There, in the middle of an empty road, directly in my path, a rocky wall on either side blocking any apparent way in or out, was a turtle.

As turtles do, it stared at me unblinking, before shaking its head, I swear, and withdrawing into its shell to wait for the stranger to pass. This I did, and not fifty feet later on this road was an exit. Dare I add that as I crested the last hill, I saw the Acropolis from an unobstructed vantage, dramatically backlit by afternoon lightning bolts as if thrown by Zeus himself? Was he pleased?

Displeased? Or perhaps merely impatient to be rid of a bumbling foreigner? I did not wait for an answer.

Finding I was only yards from "civilization," I walked down a pleasant residential street and finally found what I dubbed "Museum of Technology #2," though it is actually the senior of the two. This museum, which shared space with an abstract art exhibit in a (deliberately?) thought-provoking and somewhat incongruous contrast to prosaic gears, siphons, and pulleys, was smaller and emphasized military technology—the ancient equivalent of an arms race. But ... it also boasted a wine-pouring female robot.

Robots, it appears, will always be popular.

It is difficult to know if ancient Greeks had the time or inclination to explore the philosophical ramifications of technology, beyond speculation of an easier and perhaps more humane future. Technology was seen as an improvement on human effort, not as a force unto itself. In his *Physica*, Aristotle maintained that technology imitates nature, but man had not yet landed on the moon or invented nuclear weapons capable of indescribable destruction. Nor had man created "artificial intelligence" quite capable, and inevitably certain, of outthinking its creator. "Automatons," in the Greek mind, imitated humans; they did not supplant them.

Why then do we, sophisticated beneficiaries of higher education, enjoying a global perspective, and with the benefit of history, fear technology? Whereas the ancient Greeks, in thrall to "myths" and gods, seemed to relish invention and embrace wonder? Were the Greeks merely naïve about the possible misuses of technology? Blissfully unaware of the undiscovered destructive power of technology? Incapable of fearing a loss of "privacy" no one had yet conceived?

It is impossible to know. Maybe it is enough simply to stand amazed at the sheer genius of the human mind, to admire the intelligence and skill of the ancient Greeks (and elsewhere in the ancient world). Perhaps we can speculate on "what-if's," such as "what if" the steam turbine devised by Heron of Alexandria in the first century had been built and adopted throughout the ancient world in a kind of steampunk revisionist history?

But we can rest assured there is one invention uniquely our own. Another writer emailed me from Crete during her stay there. A new museum had just opened that day, and she was the first visitor: a museum of Ancient Greek Technology. Ah, the franchise. I bet you didn't see that one coming, Aristotle.

A little boy dressed as an Evone stands with three on-duty guards

TOUGH MEN WEAR SKIRTS

Gayle McGill

A repetitive percussive clap pried my eyes away from the baking hot Athens sidewalk. A man, a very tall man marched toward me dressed in an astonishing outfit. He wore a skirt, a really short skirt—a white pleated affair that barely covered his behind. Heavy white tights covered his long legs. A finely embroidered blue vest and fluffy exaggerated trumpet-sleeved white shirt topped off the outfit. On his feet, bright red clogs with upturned toes sported enormous black pom-poms. A red tam-shaped hat with a tassel that hung down below his waist pretty perfectly matched the shoes. My mom would approve.

Every second step he raised his right leg almost shoulder height then slammed his foot hard against the pavement with the clamorous slap that alerted me to his presence. Was this for real? Was this some tourist thing? Laughter bubbled up. It was like happening upon John Cleese of Monty Python doing his silly walk in a micro mini.

The soldier marched closer. My laughter died. I caught a whiff of my own ignorance. The precision of his step, his upright posture, fierce focus and very real looking rifle made me realize that he for one took this march seriously. Yes, this was most certainly for real.

Fascinated, I turned and followed the soldier down Herodes

Atticus Street past the presidential mansion, past the Zappeion Gardens watching his two sets of black tasseled mid-calf garters sway with each stomped step. He stopped abruptly then slowly raised his leg straight out, pointed his toe and bent the leg in a pawing-like swing, his heavy red shoes grazing the pavement. My newfound cultural sensitivity forced me to kill my laughter. It was a struggle. He then reverted to his right leg stomp until at a set of heavy ornate gates he made a sharp turn. Two soldiers in perfectly normal fatigues sprang forward to open the gates and my mini-skirted soldier marched through the opening out of sight but not out of mind.

It is more than forty years since that day, and I've returned to Athens to write a story about these soldiers, the Evzones, and to explore the role that they have played in Greek history from the time of Homer to modern day.

"Run," I bellow at my husband as we dash across Syntagma Square toward the courtyard of the Presidential Palace on an I-can't-believe-it-is-this-hot-already Sunday morning. We've already taken a wrong turn navigating from our Airbnb, and I'm hell-bent on seeing two full platoons of Evzones plus marching band do their Sunday morning eleven o'clock changing of the guard in full ceremonial uniform.

Tourists line the square. I'm at the back and can't see a damn thing, but I can certainly hear the soldiers approach. The crowd surges, and I glimpse a pom-pommed red clog that I now know is called a *tsarouhi* and I also know why it makes such a racket. These soldiers are slamming down an eight-pound custom-made leather shoe with sixty nails on the bottom. It is meant to sound like battle, like freedom, like independence—and it does. And that white-pleated skirt I found so hilarious is called a *foustanela*. It is custom tailored from thirty-three yards of fabric with four hundred pleats, one for each year of the Turkish occupation. The color white symbolizes the purity of the national struggles. And so it goes. Each part of the uniform is exquisitely made and laden with significance.

I catch only snippets of the changing of the guard and their slow motion high-legged *pas de deux* that I've pretty much memorized from YouTube videos. The platoons turn onto Herodes Atticus Street for the march back to the barracks. The crowd thins but I, drenched in sweat, keep pace and follow the soldiers with a giddy excitement. I'm buoyed by their energy and the ferocious sound of their steps. How beautiful the soldiers are. All tall, all slim, all young. But still the uniform makes me smile. I'm not pleased with my progress on this front and know that if they start with that pointy-toed-slap-walk thing I won't be able be to keep a straight face.

For the second time, forty years later, I stand by the barrack's ornate gates and watch the soldiers pivot right and disappear into the barracks.

The next day I scour the absolutely wonderful Benaki Museum, and the day after, the just as marvelous National Archeology Museum for early images of men in pleated skirts. I find them galore—on vases, sculptures, mosaics, jewelry and most wonder-fully in the costume section of the Benaki. There is a white pleated skirt from Crete that is knee length, while some of the sculptures as early as fifth century BCE show skirts so short that the soldier's genitals are exposed. Interesting battle strategy.

For the next several days my husband and I tour the mainland sites of Mycenae, Olympia and the jewel of them all, Delphi. In each place, I ask any Greek who will listen what they think of the

Evzones. Is it not cruel that the soldiers have to stand motionless in the hot sun in that heavy uniform? What do they think of the elaborate costume and curious marching? Do they think maintaining the Evzones is a good use of tax dollars?

The soldiers are hand-picked and considered elite, they tell me, and are trained to stand motionless and tolerate the heat. It is a great honor to serve. They did not question the Evzone purpose. No one seemed to find the uniform or the march the least bit silly.

Did I know that Homer mentioned the Evzone warriors over 2,800 years ago? I'm told that many view the Evzone as a symbol of the struggle against the Ottoman occupation that ended in 1821, and they are still sometimes called *tsoliades* after the ragged but fierce anti-Ottoman insurgents who fought the Turks in rural Greece. One guide told me a story about World War II when the Germans entered Athens. They ordered the Evzone guarding the Acropolis to lower the Greek flag and raise the Swastika. He did, but instead of handing over the Greek flag, he wrapped himself in it and jumped off of the Acropolis to his death. Another tells me that Syntagma Square has been the site of many protests recently, and that the Evzones have stood unflinching through riots, tear gas and even Molotov cocktails.

Back in Athens I get a different opinion from the desk clerk at my hotel. The Evzones, he said, are an absurd, irrelevant anachronism—guarding a government they don't even respect. Fair enough, but I'm startled by my surge of protectiveness toward the Evzones.

A week has passed, and today is my big day. For the third time, I stand nervously at Two Herodes Atticus Street in front of the ornate gates, this time waiting to be admitted to the barracks for an interview with Lieutenant Nikolaos Leontaris and Evzone Private Konstantinos Bantounas. A well-connected fellow writer put me in touch with a Navy commander who with great attentiveness and courtesy got the ball rolling, and after many emails and phone calls, an interview time was arranged. I cannot believe my good fortune.

Lieutenant Leontaris escorts me through the gates and across a sunny courtyard where two Evzones stand motionless. They are wearing the khaki summer uniform. In the background I hear marching and orders being shouted. On the second floor of the barracks, I sit at a table in a small light-filled auditorium. I spy a copy of the interview questions that I emailed the lieutenant the day before. Excellent.

The walls are covered with posters, photographs and drawings of Evzones in different eras. On tables near the front of the room various bits and pieces of the Evzone and officer uniforms are laid out in a colorful display. At the back of the room, large glass cases contain mannequins dressed in the three different Evzone uniforms—the white ceremonial, the khaki summer and the royal blue winter uniforms. There is also the blue Cretan uniform with its white knee-high boots and the Evzone officer's uniform with its knee-length *foustanela* and red-and-gold vest called a *fermeli*. All in all an exquisite feast for the eyes. Lieutenant Leonartis shows me each piece. We chat easily. His English is fluent, and I enjoy his obvious pride in the fineness of the garments.

A very tall young man in fatigues enters the room. I'm introduced to Private Konstantinos Bantounas. I see that he has the physical characteristics to be an Evzone. The requirements state that the soldier must be from six-foot-one inch to six-foot-nine inches and have a fine body displacement. Private Bantounas stands an impressive six-foot-six, is twenty-six years old, and a university finance graduate. He has wanted to be an Evzone since he was six years old. His brother was also an Evzone. His parents are proud.

I'm surprised to learn that all Greek men are conscripted for nine months to a year of military service, officers for two to five years. Some soldiers opt to take an additional six weeks of training to become an Evzone. Only forty-five percent make it through the training.

Evzones work in pairs. They are physically matched and practice synchronizing their march. They also help each other dress which, for the white ceremonial uniform, can take up to an hour.

Private Bantounas is about to transition to the role of observer. An observer monitors each Evzone on duty for signs of distress and can relieve the guard of his post if he is in danger. I've seen observers almost tenderly wipe the sweat from the face of an Evzone, smooth out the long tassel from his cap or adjust his uniform and murmur encouragements. An Evzone may smack the butt of his riffle on the ground to signal that he needs help and answer yes or no questions with eye blinks.

Private Konstantinos tells me that being an Evzone is the hardest thing he has ever done and expects it will be the hardest thing he will ever have to do. An Evzone must endure many states of physical pain. He believes that this has strengthened his character.

"Has there been any consideration given to changing the uniform so that it is not as demanding?" I ask.

"No," Lieutenant Leonartis emphatically states. "The uniform dates back to the Chlamys worn since the time of Homer. This uniform was worn by the heroes that every nation needs—the heroes that fought the revolution. It honors our ancestors."

"You see, even their movements are symbolic," says Lieutenant Leonartis. "There is meaning behind every move."

The Lieutenant says something to Private Bantounas in Greek.

The Evzone springs to his feet and suddenly I know exactly what is coming—the pointy-toed-slap-walk that I found so hilarious years ago. *Do not laugh. Do not blow this,* I beg myself.

"You see how he raises his leg?" Private Konstantinos raises his leg and indeed does the pointy-toed-slap-walk. "His legs make the shape of a four symbolizing the four hundred years of Ottoman occupation."

I blush. I do smile, but it is a sheepish smile.

"Would you ever shoot your gun?" I ask Private Konstantinos.

"No," he responds. "My job is to stand still whatever happens and to stay still. When I am in uniform and on duty I am no longer a human. I am a symbol that honors our ancestors. Often, people stand silent for a minute to honor the dead. We stand silent for an hour."

"It is important to keep the Evzone tradition," adds Lieutenant Leontaris. "It connects the past, present and maybe even the future. Symbols are crucial for a nation. If you keep symbols in history you keep memories alive. The Evzone symbols helped us maintain our values through the occupation and still do to this day. The symbols are alive."

The symbols are alive. I sit quietly, awed by their eloquence. I finally understand.

I'm back in Oakland now. I often think of the Evzones and meeting Lieutenant Leontaris and Private Konstantinos. When they accompanied me back to the gates after the interview, Private Konstantinos suggested a detour. We stopped in front of an old black-and-white photograph. It is the photograph that accompanies this story. In the picture, a little boy dressed as an Evzone stands in front of three guards on duty, dreaming of the day he, too, will become an Evzone. My eyes brimmed with tears. Just as Private

Konstantinos must have done, I thought. There it was in black and white—a picture of the unbroken Greek spirit—the hand from the past that lives in the present and guides the future.

I imagine the soldiers standing motionless in rain or even snow. I picture them in the cold dark night with no one watching, solemnly guarding democracy. Silently paying homage to the heroes of the past. There is a kind of comfort in that thought.

For me, the jury is in—the men in skirts rock. Greece is all the richer for maintaining this symbol and understanding its value. And for the rest of us, what an added bonus that this tradition is expressed with the wonderous Evzone uniforms, the meditative slow dance of the changing of the guard, the highly symbolic pointy-toed-slap-walk and their fierce march that rings through the streets of Athens, and I hope always will.

The Temple of Athena's Porch of the Maidens at the Acropolis

The Pantheon of Me

Daphne Beyers

Like fleet-footed Artemis, I darted past the multilingual crowd loitering at the entrance to the Acropolis of Athens. With the temperature rising, mid-afternoon was a most unwise time of day to visit the Parthenon, my inner Athena whispered. Fortunately, the goddess of strategy had devised my itinerary that day. Avoiding the entrance and the crowds, I continued along the wide pedestrian boulevard until I came to a boulder rising off the side of the Acropolis. I climbed to the top and took in a panoramic view of Athens, five hundred feet below me. Square white buildings, tiny in the distance, stretched out as far as the eye could see. Interspersed between the buildings I saw dark green foliage that could be shrubs or trees.

Twenty-five hundred years ago when the sculptor Phidias built the Parthenon on this rocky outcrop above Athens, the view would have been remarkably similar. There would have been fewer houses and more trees. No phone lines or electric cables. Possibly more goats meandering about. Maybe some oxen. No paved streets. No cars or scooters.

Okay, modern Athens has changed quite a bit since ancient days, but despite these changes, there was something timeless in that far-seeing view from my perch. Perhaps it was the way the sunlight fell across the city stretched below, or the tall, verdant hills in the distance that formed a natural boundary that had been there since ancient days, or the consistent blue of the Mediterranean sky. Sun, hills, sky, all would have appeared much the same to Phidias as they did to me, a wandering tourist of the twenty-first century. I could imagine how such an unchanging land would give rise to a pantheon of equally unchanging, immortal gods.

The ancient Greek gods, called Olympians because of their residence on Mount Olympus in northern Greece, dominated ancient Greek culture for thousands of years. *Where are the gods now?* I wondered. The rise of Christian monotheism ended the long cultural reign of the Olympians, but did it also end the gods themselves or did they merely fade from sight?

Just as the Parthenon transformed over the centuries from a temple to Athena to a Christian church, there is evidence of the ancient Greek gods morphing into Christian saints. There is even speculation that the dying and reborn Sumerian fertility god Tammuz morphed into the ancient Greek god Adonis who in turn became the Christian Jesus with his seasonal rebirth ritual. In his book *The Hero with a Thousand Faces*, comparative mythologist Joseph Campbell traced what he called the monomyth of the hero's journey across ancient cultures worldwide. Campbell posits that these myths emerge naturally from human consciousness or from what the twentieth- century psychoanalyst Carl Jung called the "collective unconscious" shared by all humanity. If this was so, are the ancient Greek gods present in our modern-day culture?

Unlike the strange animal-headed gods of ancient Egypt, the Olympic gods with their vanity, sibling rivalry, and power struggles are entirely relatable to modern people. The lead characters of one of the twenty-first century's most popular television series, HBO's *Game of Thrones*, closely resemble the ancient Greek gods Hephaestus, Ares, and Aphrodite. Tyrion, a dwarf on the show, is a modern day Hephaestus, the ancient Greek's dwarfish, crippled god of fire and engineering. Tyrion engineers siege weapons and uses fire to defeat an enemy attack. Tyrion's brother Jaime is a modern day Ares, the ancient Greek god of war. In the *Iliad,* the epic poem of the Trojan War, Ares is depicted as impetuous, easily provoked to anger, undisciplined and chaotic. In *Game of Thrones*, Jaime is depicted in a similar way, and his impetuous violence starts a multi-sided civil war. Lastly, Jaime's twin sister Cersei follows the archetype of Aphrodite, the ancient Greek goddess of love and beauty. Cersei uses her beauty to manipulate her way to power. She has an illicit love affair with her twin brother Jaime just as Aphrodite had an illicit affair with Ares. Cersei's vanity starts the civil war on the television show just as Aphrodite's vanity is blamed for starting the Trojan War.

Are we simply telling the same stories over and over, dressing them up in new costumes and giving them new names? If the Greek gods live on in our modern-day entertainment, they have not disappeared. *So where are they now?* I wondered again.

Loud-thundering Zeus of the dazzling lightning bolt woke me from my reverie at the edge of the Acropolis. I had been so lost in my thoughts I hadn't noticed the dark clouds gathering above. Taking note of my surroundings, I realized the tall boulder I had climbed to get a better view not only jutted out over the precipice, it was one of the highest features around. I was sticking out like a lightning rod. Not the best place to be during a thunderstorm. A flash of lightning and a simultaneous clap of thunder crashed so close I felt static in my hair and smelled the sharp discharge of ozone.

I may be a first world tourist living in the third age of modernity, but I was as helpless before the storm's fury as the ancient inhabitants. Zeus towered above me in a thundercloud and threw down his lightning bolts in an asymmetric display of power. My sneakers slipped on the rock's worn surface made smooth, almost glassy, by countless tourists before me. The wind gusted, and I felt the first drops of rain. If I were still up there when the rain came in earnest, the rock's already slick surface would become a slippery death trap.

I was caught between Scylla and Charybdis, those ancient Greek monsters Odysseus had to navigate. On the one hand, I needed to get down quickly before a lightning bolt blasted me. On the other hand, I had to go slowly enough not to slip and fall to my death. Like Odysseus, I chose Scylla, the lesser of the two evils. Where Charybdis was certain death, Scylla offered Odysseus at least the chance of survival. For me, speeding down the rock's slick surface was certain death. Instead, I crouched down and began to lower myself inch by careful inch using hand and footholds and trusting neither very much.

I made it back to the pedestrian boulevard alive. As soon as my feet touched solid ground, the storm clouds dispersed as if satisfied by my retreat. Did my flight from the pinnacle assuage Zeus's wrath? I was down among the mortal tourists again, where I belonged, my temporary elevation abandoned. Had I inadvertently challenged the gods by climbing so high above my mortal station? Was I guilty of hubris, that most dire of ancient taboos wherein a person's pride or arrogance makes them think themselves equal to the gods?

If I had strayed into hubris, it was only a momentary error. I was not actually struck down by lightning. Our modern-day worldview influenced by science says there is a natural cause to all natural phenomena. That was not Zeus up in the sky but negatively charged ions in the clouds meeting positively charged ions from the earth and sparking an electrical surge as lightning. No gods required. We've replaced capricious gods with a more predicable though still chaotic nature, a god's personal wrath with impersonal nonlinear dynamics. That seems reasonable in theory, but when nature comes after you hurling thunderbolts, it's hard not to take it personally.

Which brings us back to Joseph Campbell and the ancient world of gods and myths. Joseph Campbell believed life by itself is meaningless. We bring life meaning. Our consciousness, our conscious experience of life is what gives life meaning. This is the mystical view of life where the omens and oracles of the ancient Greeks reside. It is the world of synchronicity, the theory the psychoanalyst Carl Jung proposed as an "acausal connecting principle."

Causality is the scientific theory that all events in the natural world have a natural cause. If you come across a flower growing by a lake, God or Zeus or some other supernatural force did not put it there magically. A natural cause should be looked for. In this case, a seed must have landed there, and the flower grew from that seed. The causal connection between seed and flower can be proven repeatedly by finding the right kind of seed, planting it, and observing as it grows into a flower.

Perhaps the seed was dropped by a bird that was startled by a fox that was chased by hunting dogs owned by a prince who was daydreaming about his true love and longing to find the most beautiful flower in the world to give her. While all that might have happened, none of it has a causal connection to the flower because as long as the right seed is planted, the flower will grow without need of a bird or fox or hunting dogs or a daydreaming prince.

In Carl Jung's theory of synchronicity, events that can be traced through a natural chain of cause and effect can also have an acausal connection that gives the events added psychological meaning independent of their physical causality. While the natural world may be driven by impersonal, chaotic or deterministic forces; the human psyche assembles the experience of the natural world through a deeper, archetypal pattern of meaning.

The example Jung gives of synchronicity happened when he was treating a patient who had the night before dreamed of a golden scarab. When Jung's patient mentioned the dream during the therapy session, an insect collided with the window. When Jung opened the window, he discovered the insect was a golden scarab rarely seen in that climate. This was not just an outlandish coincidence. It was a meaningful coincidence. The golden scarab's journey to Carl Jung's window could be traced through natural cause and effect, but its arrival at the window at the precise moment the patient described her dream demonstrated a psychologically meaningful connection outside of physical causality.

The ancient Greek myth of Zeus hurling thunderbolts is not made false because we now know all about positive and negative ions. My psychological experience of the thunderstorm contained a lot more meaning than the impersonal interactions of colliding ions. What deep forces brought me to that rocky pinnacle just as the thunderstorm began? Was it coincidence or synchronicity? I had been pondering the gods and asking myself, *Where are they now?* And just then a lightning bolt flashed in the sky and thunder shook the earth. Did Zeus reveal himself in answer to my question?

Scientists would argue thunderstorms commonly occur in Athens at that time of day, and they are not wrong to argue that. Synchronicity does not deny causality. What synchronicity does do is bring the living consciousness of the human observer into the equation. Science has brought the modern world many advances in terms of health, longevity, reduced mortality rates, and many other improvements and conveniences, but as a worldview it has its drawbacks. In my opinion, the purely materialistic worldview of science posits a dead world of impersonal, natural forces, a world of unfathomable complexity, but one ultimately devoid of meaning. A falling star is just a rock from space, and a rock is dead matter.

In the ancient Greek world of gods and goddesses, myths and legends, the world was alive and full of mystery. In the ancient world trees, stones, brooks, even the sun and stars were alive with gods and spirits. A falling star was a prophetic sign sent by the Titan Asteria, the goddess of nighttime divinations. In the ancient worldview, consciousness was not merely a by-product of a chemical process in the brain, nor was it relegated to only happening within the human observer. The world itself was alive, conscious, and aware.

It is not the world that has changed; it is we who have changed. We've traded a world of wonder, full of gods and spirits, for a dead world of modern conveniences. We live longer, but our lives are less meaningful. The world is just as alive now as it was in ancient Greece, if only we could learn again to hear the voice of Zeus hidden in the thunder, saying, "I am here."

Stacked-rock altar with devotional statues

REVISITING THE ANCIENT GODS

Donna Hemmila

The trail ran cold at the Prison of Socrates.

I studied the three iron-barred cells carved into the rock hillside and the tangle of dirt paths branching away from them. My cell-phone photo of the rudimentary map posted at the park entrance offered no guidance. Nothing on it resembled the landscape stretched before me. I was lost, confused, and admittedly faint of heart.

I'd ventured to Athens' Filopappou Hill in search of the old gods, or rather the modern Greeks who still worship them. It was Summer Solstice, the longest day, and LABRYS, a Hellenistic religious community, was gathering for a celebration ritual. I was intrigued and, at that moment of uncertain location, a bit apprehensive.

I'd read accounts of tourists being mugged on Filopappou Hill, even when traveling in groups. There I was in an isolated, wooded area alone. Only the year before, a young man fell to his death from a cliff during a run-in with robbers. My adventurous self wanted to push onward. My wimpy self wanted to slink back to my hotel. I decided to push on.

After imploring Athena to guide my path forward, I set out on the one trail that wound up the hillside. At the very least, I would find a magnificent sunset view of the Acropolis and the Saronic Gulf that kisses the feet of the sprawling city.

Surrounded on every side by the magnificent ruins of the civilization their ancestors built, I could understand how modern-day Greeks would embrace their old religion, although those who do are a small minority.

Some ninety-five percent of the population belongs to the Christian Orthodox faith. It wasn't until 2017 that the Supreme Council of Ethnic Hellenes, an organization dedicated to the restoration of Greek polytheism, gained legal recognition as a "known religion" for those communities that worship the ancient Greek gods. "Known religion" status allows polytheism practioners to build places of worship and openly perform ceremonies.

The LABRYS religious community, founded in 2008, has a worship center in Athens and conducts public ceremonies at the temples of Zeus in Nemea and Athens and on Filopappou Hill, following the ancient practice of worshipping outdoors. The group professes to promote piety, justice, and kinship—not qualities I'd associate with the likes of Zeus, Poseidon and the rest of the violently vindictive Olympians.

I've always had a low opinion of these old gods. The summer I taught a World Mythology class did nothing to change my mind. I was working part-time at a community college when I got a call from the chair of the English department.

"I hear you'll teach anything," he said.

Regretfully, the faculty member scheduled to teach the mythology course realized he could make more money giving tennis lessons for the summer. Would I be willing to step in? The department chair desperately argued his case. Classes started in a week.

Never one to let lack of qualification hold me back, I accepted his offer. Thus began my mad, crash course in centuries of unfamiliar myths from dozens of disparate civilizations. After I met my students, I realized I was overthinking the *world* aspect of the course. Try as I might to interest them in the Hindu creation stories and the clever exploits of gentle Native American gods, they were obsessed with the familiar tales of the ancient Olympians. Despite my disdain for their tendencies toward violence and destruction, I had to admit the old Greek gods made for good storytelling.

About three weeks into the class, a student asked the question I'd been dreading.

"So is the Bible a myth?" an earnest young man challenged.

I had no desire to embroil the class in a heated debate about true religion. After acknowledging that the Bible contained people, places and events rooted in history, I offered the only words of wisdom I could muster.

"No culture, no people, thinks of its religious belief as a myth," I told the class. "We need to respect everyone's right to believe what they believe."

That was the best answer I could come up with back then and to this day, twenty years later. I reminded myself of this as I trudged up the hillside.

Eventually, I came upon a small clearing near the summit of Filopappou Hill where a man was stacking rocks in a pile.

"*Yassas*," I greeted him with the one word I knew in Greek. "I'm looking for this place." I showed him the cellphone map. "Do you know where this is?"

"It is here," he said, sweeping his hand across the clearing.

"Is there a solstice ceremony tonight?"

"Yes, yes, it is here."

"Would it be all right if I attended?"

"Of course, of course. Welcome, welcome."

We were both speaking English strangely—me slowly enunciating every syllable and he repeating everything twice, the way people do when they are not sure their listener understands them.

As he continued stacking rocks, others arrived, bearing ritual objects, including a clay jug; incense burner; a replica of an ancient labrys, the two-headed axe from which the group took its name; and small plaster statues of Athena, Aphrodite, Apollo and Hermes. They arranged these statues of the gods atop the stone altar the man had built. Then they helped him complete a circle of stacked rocks about two feet high. A woman, dressed in a white robe draped with a long, diaphanous scarf the color of the Aegean Sea, spread a bright orange and gold cloth on a flat rock serving as a table. On it she arranged the clay jug and platters of cookies and cakes.

"How many are coming?" I asked.

The rock builder shrugged.

"It doesn't matter. If we are just one, that is enough."

"What are you doing here?" A young woman approached me, her tone curious, her English perfect.

Unlike the older women gathering, she did not dress in ancient Greek costume. She wore black cutoffs and a T-shirt with a collection of Celtic and Viking pendants around her neck. Her name was Despoina and she was twenty-four. She'd joined LABRYS to reclaim her Greek heritage and culture. She liked the idea of worshipping in nature, like the Vikings and other pagan peoples.

"We're not pagans," one of the men corrected her. "We're Hellenists."

"We're Hellenists," Despoina repeated.

Discreetly I pulled out the silver Celtic protection knot pendant I wore under my shirt.

"I love it!" she yelled enthusiastically.

From that moment, she took me under her wing, recounting what would happen during the ritual. She ended with the disclaimer that she was not the best person to explain LABRYS since she was new to the community. I thought she was exactly the best person to explain it. She contributed passion, commitment and youthful enthusiasm. If groups like this intended to prosper, they needed young peoplelike that.

"What does your family think of you becoming part of this old religion?" I asked her. "Most Greeks are Orthodox. They don't believe in all that church stuff. They're pretty much atheists anyway."

The music of drumbeats and panpipes interrupted our conversation. Incense wafted over the altar. The ceremony had begun. About forty people of all ages, including a few children, had gathered. They converged in a circle around the clearing, and I joined them.

A man in white-and-red robes moved toward the rock altar, carrying the clay vessel. He lifted it overhead, intoning a prayer in Ancient Greek. The circle of people raised their arms to the sky. I did the same. At the end of his incantation, he poured wine from the jug into the center of the stone circle.

A procession of men and women followed him, each taking a turn in reciting a prayer and pouring offerings over the stones. I didn't understand a word of what they were saying, but the meaning was clear. These were true believers, united in honoring their gods and celebrating the community they had created.

When our circle turned outward away from the altar to face the setting sun, I felt the resonant Ancient Greek words wash over me. Inwardly I thanked Helios, the sun god, for driving his chariot across the sky and gifting the world with the beauty of the sunset. The frustrations I'd experienced during my week in Athens—the soul-crushing heat, the overcrowded Plaka with wall-to-wall tacky tourist shops, the exhaust-polluted traffic jams, the larcenous taxi drivers—all slipped away. For the first time, I felt welcomed in Greece

After the ritual ended, the elderly man I stood next to in the circle clasped my hands between his, nodding and smiling approval of my presence. Another man offered me a glass of the ceremonial wine. It was the color of cherry soda and lollipop sweet. When I saw others emptying a bit of their wine into the stone circle, I did the same.

I asked Despoina what else they had poured into the stones.

"Essential oils, herbs," she answered. "We offer these things to these entities, these gods, whatever you want to call them."

Exactly, I thought, whatever you want to call them.

I thanked the people who had shown me such welcomed kinship and made my way down the hill, this time unafraid.

Early the next morning, I left Athens to visit other ancient sites: Epidaurus, Mycenae, Olympia and Delphi. At each temple ruin, I considered the old gods in a new light. Their greatness did not manifest itself to me, but the spirit of the Greek people, ancient and modern, did. Through centuries of wars, oppression and economic hardships, they flourished, confident in the knowledge it was they who created all the civilized world holds dear. At every ancient site, I saw the magnificence of Greek art, theater, philosophy and science. If the old gods—whatever you want to call them—did not impress me, the resilience of those who choose to honor them gleamed brighter than all the gold in ancient Mycenae.

The author at the villa on Madouri

THE BOATMAN

Linda Watanabe McFerrin

What is there worth seeing any more
Except some beautiful woman
Walking in the corridor and smiling
Even if it is in a hospital
Even if it's a nurse
Even if it's not a human being
Even if it's the end
Or just before the end
In other words, the beginning

—Nanos Valaoritis, *Pan Daimonium*, 2005

"Varkáris (the boatman) will come for you." These were the only in-structions we received as we stood facing the vast blue expanse that pulsed before us.

Lawrence and I had arrived, road weary and relieved, at Lefkada, an island situated in the Ionian Sea on the west coast of Greece. Known for its connection to myth and legend—Sappho supposedly committed suicide at Cape Lefkada—the island is purported to be Homer's Ithaca, and it's said that it is in Nydri, on the island's south coast, that Odysseus's palace was located. I had, however, first become familiar with Lefkada or Lefkas, as it is often called, not as this epic setting, but as the eponymous birthplace of Lefcadio Hearn, a writer whose popularity in Japan guaranteed his work a place on my mother's bookshelf and therefore my own. But Lawrence and I had not come to Lefkas, for any of these reasons. We had come to visit our dear friend and mentor, famed poet Nanos Valaoritis on Madouri, his family's private island. It floated, a tiny green cloud barely visible from our Lefkada perch, out in the wide azure, along with other small private islands like Skorpios and Meganisi.

The journey had been a long one, hundreds of miles by bus, from Neapoli where we had once again run to escape the trauma of death and sorrow. The year was 1998. My father had died a year and a half before, days after our return from Africa, and since that time we'd been caring for my mother caught fast in the ever-advancing grip of debilitating Alzheimer's disease. In the midst of all of this, my first novel, *Namako*, roughly based on my childhood in Japan, was about to be published, and neither of my parents would be able to read it. It was a surreal time, full of highs and lows, of endings and beginnings. How had we managed it all? I don't remember. We were both working full-time and this trip to Greece seemed impossible ... as impossible, almost, as the blue of the sea.

But it was also impossible not to make the journey. Sometimes there is nothing to do but move forward. The wheels had not yet completely come off our wagon and friends were calling, offering us a reprieve, a way out, an adventure, a safe landing. We had been through a lot; we were ready for anything. Lawrence had his violin. I had my journal. And at last Varkáris (the boatman) arrived, and we were on the water even before we knew it, the salt spray cooling our faces, the wind in our hair.

What do you expect when you arrive on an island like Madouri—a personal keep floating like a dreamy raft in sea of history? Do you expect a simple neoclassical manse of sunlit ochre with a large double door fronted by wide stone steps upon which family members wait with welcoming smiles: Nanos, Marie, Katarina, Zoe with a babe in her arms and her husband Louis at her side? Do you expect large salons full of brilliant thinkers from around the world, gathered to talk about archeology and myth for days on end? Do you expect serenity; an airy bedroom, bright and inviting, in which to open your suitcases, collapse and gather strength before heading out in search of meandering paths; a dappled grove; a short climb to a small stone church deserted and under repair? Do you expect mornings full of coffee and chatter and bonhomie?

It so happened that our arrival coincided with the Institute of Archaeomythology's first International Symposium. The Institute, inspired by the multidisciplinary scholarship and approach of famed archeologist Marija Gimbutas, was founded to foster and support ongoing archaeomythological research. This initial conference, "Deepening the Disciplines," featured presentations by Cristina Biaggi, "Myth, monument and matristic societies: The Goddess in Neolithic island cultures;" Janine Canan, "A journey to the Goddess in poetry;" Alice Petrie, "Why is Delphi at Delphi?" and our host, Nanos Valaoritis, "Homer and the alphabet." The atmosphere amid the twenty or so speakers was electric, with ideas sparking new insights and sudden revelations among the assembled. Adding to this bright meeting of the minds was the energy of our hostess, talented surrealist painter and materfamilias, Marie Wilson, who had learned from and worked with other abstract and surrealist artists like Man Ray, Wilfredo Lam and Pablo Picasso in France and even entertained some, like Elisa Breton, there on the island.

Lawrence and I were enthralled and carried away by the company. Madouri had become a kind of Prospero's Isle full of voices and spirits. Like the others gathered around Nanos and his family for the occasion, we found ourselves inspired and fully engaged: laughing, dancing, penning poetry and song. Capturing the easy warmth of the whole affair, Lawrence found a moment or two near the small church on the island during which he composed a lovely air on his violin, which we came to refer to as "Madouri Swing." It has a loose, easy rhythm full of the joy that filled our days. I think not a single participant wanted to leave Madouri. In the end, it was a sudden storm that ushered us from the isle—a storm and a raucous gathering at a tavern in Lefkada, enlivened by furious fiddle music and an exciting dance by one of the organizers, both performed in a fine frenzy.

I thought about this now, years later, as we stepped from the taxi and into the searing wall-to wall-sunlight and the mad crush of pedestrian traffic in Athens' fashionable Kolonaki district.

This was another journey of miles and years, similar and yet so different from our decades-ago pilgrimage to Madouri. So much had changed in the intervening years. The Valaoritis family, with the exception of son, Dino, was now headquartered in Athens where we had to rely on cabs, not boatmen, to ferry us to their home. Marie had passed away, Nanos had been unwell for some time, and their daughters—Katarina and Zoe—were wrestling with the prospect of further loss. Still, there was something desperately familiar about it.

Now, as we made our way up the crowded streets of the Kolonaki, I thought back to that stay on the isle. Lawrence and I were again faced with trauma. Nanos, now mortally ill, had just come home from a recent hospital stay, and as we rushed toward his apartment in the intense summer heat, the two moments seemed to sizzle, surreally fracture, and join.

I don't remember if we took the elevator or the stairs to get to the family's apartment. Perhaps it was Zoe or Katarina who buzzed us in, or maybe it was one of the caregivers who whisked in and out of the rooms on their various missions, like the sprites that responded to Prospero's needs and wishes on his magical isle.

What I do remember is the rich aubergine perfume of the *moussaka* that Zoe made for our lunch. Unlike the streets below us, the rooms were quiet and cool and dark and aglow with the enormous eyes of the animals and girls watching us from Katarina's naïf paintings, which covered the walls and table surfaces. We spoke in whispers.

"He's sleeping," Zoe told us, but this did not seem to diminish in any way the comings and goings of the helpers. Louis arrived with wine, and in this fabulous and fantastic jungle of scent, image and murmurs we reminisced about art, past journeys, old dreams and new, and the way our worlds had rocked away from one another and back again.

Finally we stepped into the room where Nanos lay, his long white hair softly arranged on the pillow around him. He looked very much the same as he always looked, so wise, engaged, inquisitive. He was awake, and although he had lost his voice at the hospital, he was able to speak very softly. We had to lean in so close to hear him.

"I didn't think you would come," he whispered.

"Of course, we've come," we replied, holding his hands, wreathing him with smiles and admiration, encircling him with our memories, our love, our gratitude for all the worlds he'd shared with us through his teaching, his poetry, his friendship, his example. I'd brought him my latest book, *Navigating the Divide*, a collection of published poetry and long and short prose that had just come out. He gestured to his shelf and when someone retrieved it, he handed me his newest poetry volume: *Pan Daimonium*, another vehicle to worlds that never cease to shimmer and twist before me.

The room turned blue. The bed was a boat. Nanos was laughing that short laugh of his. Marie entered the room. He signed his book. I signed mine. His daughters were singing like sirens.

The next thing I knew Lawrence and I were out on the street, the tears, like salt spray, still in our eyes, holding hands to steady ourselves, a sea of emotion threatening to carry us away. A few weeks later we heard from Zoe that Nanos had passed away. Thankfully, we had not missed him.

Varkáris (the boatman) will come for you, I thought, *to take you somewhere new ...*
and in good time, we will join you.

Pectoral pendant of two bees, Chrysolakkos necropolis,
1800–1700 BCE

The Fat Lady of Malta

Linda Watanabe McFerrin

Madouri, Greece 1998

Sleeping lady,
we cannot call you goddess—
so say the heresy police.
"Madonna," say the men,
the emphasis on "mine."
Reclining in your egg-shaped womb,
you might be Evans' eunuch
or a deity of indeterminate sex.

Or you might just be
a bee
the archeologist saved from
certain death,
wings brine-drenched from the sea,
her palm your temple or your tomb.
Is there really any difference?

You are the wild, slow mother
tending your long tracts of subterranean cells.
Mistress of hibernation and regeneration,
princess of the hexagon,
small wonder you have spread,
come up from Africa,
crossed the Aegean,
sweetened the mead in Ireland and Wales.

Here, on Madouri,
where the cicadas rub legs in an ecstasy
of mad, shamanic rattling
under grey olive
on the salt breeze laced with mountain thyme,
they deconstruct the past
and conjure you unwittingly.

Come down from the church,
bee goddess—
wasp-waisted,
spiral-eyed—
on your multivalent wings.

The party's not over until the fat lady sings.

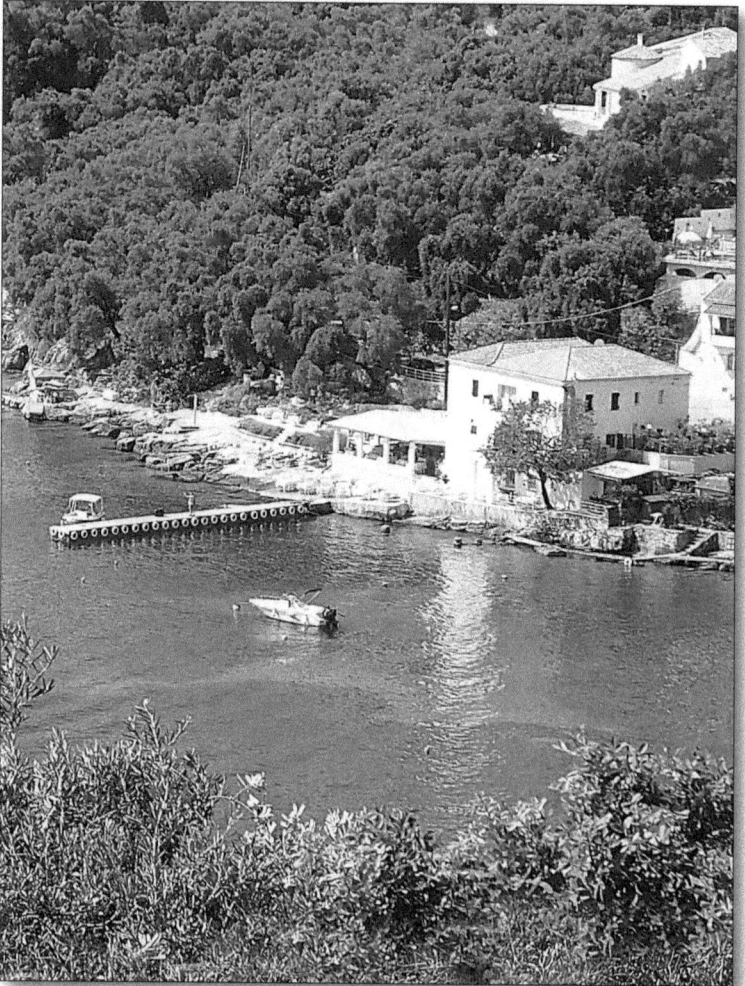
The white house on Corfu
where young Larry and Nancy Durrell lived

HAPPY AS LARRY

Joanna Biggar

The blue had already begun. As our boat rounded the turn into Kalami Bay, the white house with its third story and balcony hung invitingly over the water just as it had in my imagination. At last I had come to the lush and sun-kissed Ionian isle of Corfu (or Kerkyra) to find its magic for myself. The magic that had been implanted long ago by the irresistible words of Lawrence Durrell. And of the four houses that the legendary Durrell family had lived in during their stay on Corfu, this house on the rocky northeastern part of the island was the one he and his beautiful blonde wife Nancy had moved into to find solitude, to swim, sail, sunbathe nude, to write and paint. It is also the only one open to the public. My husband and I had come on a small tour boat to get our first glimpse approaching by sea, just as the Durrells had done.

As a welcome breeze rippled the water, the opening lines of *Prospero's Cell*, Durrell's first and most lyrical island book, about Corfu and published in 1945, came back to me.

> Somewhere between Calabria and Corfu the blue really begins. All the way across Italy you find yourself moving through a landscape severely domesticated—each valley

laid out after the architect's pattern, brilliantly lighted, human. But once you strike out from the flat and desolate Calabrian mainland towards the sea, you are aware of a change in the heart of things; aware of the horizon beginning to stain at the rim of the world; aware of *islands* coming out of the darkness to meet you.

In the morning you wake to the taste of snow on the air, and climbing the companion-ladder, suddenly enter the penumbra of shadow cast by the Albanian mountains—each wearing its cracked crown of snow— desolate and repudiating stone.

...Other countries may offer you discoveries in manners or love or landscape; Greece offers you something harder—the discovery of yourself.

On that boat from Calabria to Corfu in March 1935 were Larry, as he was called, and his bride Nancy. Née Nancy Myers, she was an art student he had met in London at the Slade School of Fine Art. The aspiring young writer and painter lived a bohemian life together for two years before being persuaded in 1935 by an English friend, George Wilkerson, to join him on green and gorgeous Corfu. Particularly seduced by Wilkerson's news that the recently married could travel by Italian train for a reduction of eighty percent, they quickly married and departed. The entire Durrell tribe—including youngest son Gerald, whose beloved accounts of their uproarious life there would become international bestsellers— soon followed. But the young couple was intent on creating their own lives. His first book, *The Pied Piper of Lovers*, with a cover painted by Nancy, was published while they journeyed to Greece. He was twenty-three. Buoyed by this success, he kept writing. Drawing on their island existence, his work portrayed a kind of paradise, one made up from myth, imagination, literature, and the whole cloth of their actual lives. It was a paradise constructed around young love. In my old age, I hoped to glimpse the enchantment—the romance of place entwined with love—of Durrell's Corfu. Still, given the tragedies I knew that had followed those blissful years, I wondered: Could such enchantment endure?

I was ready to believe, too, as we explored the city of Corfu, and found ourselves in places that might have been pages from his book. The Venetian architecture with arches on the main square reminiscent of the rue de Rivoli in Paris; the majestic "Venetian blue and gold" colors attenuated by the red, yellow and pink light falling on the houses above the port. Sitting under those arches sipping coffee while watching the tourists, we saw the passing Corfiots who might have been recent incarnations of Durrell's characters. We also followed the twisting old streets he described, with shops, cafes, restaurants—to be sure more prosperous and busy than in the 1930's—but a place still recognizable beneath the veneer of modernity.

Still, beyond the myths and magical landscapes that Durrell conjured, there was his private life, with larger-than-life characters, family drama, sketches of hardy peasants, and at its center, love. Seeking that private place, we returned to Kalami and the white house, "set like a dice on a rock, already vulnerable with scars of wind and water."

This time, instead of coming by boat, exploring the port and diving into the sea, we came by car, to visit the white house in search of its long-gone inhabitants. The winding road from the town to the village offered glimpses into many scenes from various Durrell books—and the prosperity that followed. After visiting the two rooms the young couple had originally rented in the fisherman's house and perusing memorabilia, we sat on a shaded balcony to dine: Eggplant, dolmas, sea bass, local cheese and white wine—the Durrell's world came quickly into view.

In April 1937, Durrell writes, they took those rooms after consulting a fortuneteller. All was as she predicted: "White house, white rock, friends, and a narrow style of loving; and perhaps a book that will grow out of these scraps...." The friends began with the "fine creatures," fisherman Anastasius and his wife Helen. Helen "is beautifully formed in a deep silken olive-colour," and their lovely daughters have "deep black hair which shines out in sudden hints of blue."

On that balcony, it was easy to envision all their comings and goings, expanded by other characters in their circle. Ivan Zarian, for example, with his impressive mane of hair, who intones his latest love song while claiming to be Armenia's greatest living poet. Or the marvelous doctor, Theodore Stephanides, with his fine head and golden beard, the "arcane professor of broken bones," who is also a naturalist with a deep knowledge of all things Corfiot. Lingering over coffee, we chatted about the characters we had met in just a week—the young driver hellbent to kill us by taking every corner at ninety kph; the friendly proprietor in the shabby family-owned hotel whose free drinks came with history lessons; the zany ship captain who warned about the "pull of Albania" whose dominating mountains would reset our phones with the wrong time. Durrell's outsized characters still lived.

Opening *Prospero's Cell*, I turned to another, intimate passage. Outside the white house are the singing olive trees, the coughing goats; inside, we see a bowl of wild roses, Greek cigarettes, and Nancy in a cone of yellow light cutting cheese and washing grapes. "A single candle burning upon a table between our happy selves," he writes.

But I know from what followed, the idyll of happy selves did not last. Harsh winds from Albania presaged destruction and the war to come. Also, beyond that flame of candlelight, fissures of personal destruction were to open soon.

In August 1937, the couple left for a several-months stay in Paris. He had been invited by his literary hero and mentor, Henry Miller, who would personally see to the publication of Larry's first major novel, *The Black Book*. Miller also himself gave Nancy quiet confidence by encouraging her art. And Miller's lover, the great diarist Anais Nin, would comment on Nancy's Garboesque beauty, her reticence, her stillness.

But according to Nancy's daughter by a second marriage, Joanna Hodgkin, the observed "stillness" was a forced silence caused by Larry who bullied her.

After returning to Corfu, the unravelling of Eden came quickly. In 1939, on the brink of war, the Durrell family fled Corfu and dispersed. Larry and Nancy first went to Athens, where their daughter, Penelope, was born in 1940. The Germans, following the Italians, invaded Greece in 1941. The Durrells, their infant daughter in a pannier basket, "wrapped like a loaf of bread," seeking escape to Crete, crowded into an overloaded caique. It sheltered close to cliffs during the day to avoid German bombardment, and chugged out to sea by night, emitting a dangerous trail of sparks. Once safely on Crete, they soon left for Egypt.

In Cairo as refugees, they endured more strains, and the fault lines in the marriage cracked open. Nancy and Penelope fled with other civilians to Jerusalem, and from there wrote to Larry that she was leaving him. She met journalist Edward Hodgkin, married him in 1947, and they resettled in England. Larry, meanwhile, moved to Alexandria and there met Eve Cohen, who would be the model for the first book, *Justine*, in his most acclaimed series, *The Alexandria Quartet*. Larry was also remarried in 1947, to Eve Cohen, the second of his four wives. Although the path ahead for him was paved with literary fame and fortune, it also was strewn with grief: the losses of war and family tragedies that included divorce, death and suicide.

But does the end rewrite the beginning? According to Bel Mooney, writing in the *Independent*: "Surely most couples experience their own Eden even if the snake soon slithers into sight…Their bohemian idyll couldn't last, but later bitterness could never entirely tarnish its truth for either of them."

Writing of her mother's first marriage, Joanna Hodgkin agrees. "They were amateurs and got it wrong, but she did glimpse something magical in those years." And recalling Nancy's complex feelings for Larry says that the only time she saw her mother cry was upon learning of the death of his third wife, Claude-Marie Vincedon. "Who will look after him now?" Nancy blurted, bursting into tears.

Nancy never returned to Corfu, fearing a sense of loss and disillusionment. For Larry, it was different. He already seemed to have revisited their marriage and aspects of Corfu with the publication in 1960 of *Clea*, the last novel of his quartet. Clea, the title character is beautiful, mysterious, blonde and an artist who sails, swims and sunbathes in the water with caves off Alexandria that much resemble Corfu.

Six years after publication of *Clea*, and nearly twenty since he had fled, Durrell did return to Corfu. He gave an account in an article, "Oil for the Saint; Return to Corfu," in *Holiday*, October 1966. It was a triumphal return, for now he was a celebrity who had brought good fortune to the Corfiots. But he also feared losses, memories, ghosts. "Here, too, I had made my first convulsive attempts on literature, learned to sail, been in love," he writes. As he rounded the bend to see the white house, he worried that it would still be in ruins from the bombing and the past all but dissolved. He already knew that Helen of the beautiful olive skin had died of starvation in 1940, but had saved her daughters. Then he saw the house rebuilt and his peasant friends lined up to greet him. After revisiting it all, including the cove where he and Nancy had dived so many times, he found only pleasure, not nostalgia nor false regrets. And he concluded he didn't really come back, because in many ways he had never left.

So, did it endure, this idyll of love and magical landscape? I reread the last page of *Prospero's Cell* as Durrell describes their hurried leave-taking in 1939.

> The day war was declared we stood on the balcony of the white house in a green rain straight out of heaven on to the glassy floor of the lagoon; we were destroying papers and books, packing clothes, emptying cupboards, both absorbed in the inner heart of the dark crystal, and as yet not conscious of separation.
> ...Seen through the transforming lens of memory the past seemed so enchanted that even thought would be unworthy of it.

Clearly the time of Nancy and Larry's "happy selves" had ended, but for a brief period, they were true. And, as I conjure the image of the white house, the green rain, the lagoon below, and the towering mountains of Albania, I believe through the transforming lens of his writing, the lost paradise of youth can in fact endure.

Corfu's Old Venetian Fortress

AUTHENTIC CORFU

Donna Hemmila

I'd like to claim British television has not a whit of influence on my travels, but that would be a lie. Ever since Louisa Durrell trekked across my flat screen in the ITV version of 1935 Corfu, the island cast its spell over me.

As the real-life Louisa's real son Lawrence Durrell described the island, it is the place where the blue begins. Floating dreamily in the Ionian Sea, Kerkyra—the Greek name for Corfu—beckoned with exquisite beaches, flaming bougainvillea, and skies melting a color wheel of blues into the horizon.

I had to go.

Like many a foreign invader before me, I arrived by sea: a twenty-two-hour ferry ride from Venice. When I disembarked at the ferry terminal, I so wanted a Spiros, like in the TV series, who would drive me around the island for free, find an aging villa with a sea view for me to live in, and profess his undying love until his wife returned from Athens.

Instead, I found a twenty-something driver whose main attributes were a perfect command of English and biceps hefty enough to handle my bags. I enjoyed my first look at Corfu through the windows of his taxi. So far, the island gave me everything I'd hoped for. Except the heat.

With temperatures in the 90s, I had trouble affecting a cool, stiff-upper-lip British countenance. By the time I arrived at my charming apartment-hotel on the outskirts of the city of Corfu, I was dripping in sweat and a bit wobbly on my feet. Sitting by the pool downing mineral water did not cure my lightheadedness.

As soon as I entered my room, in true British lady fashion, I shuttered the windows and took to my bed, vowing to begin my explorations of authentic Corfu early the next morning.

Little did I know, finding the *authentic* Corfu would prove more difficult than I had anticipated. Just about every major power through time has left an imprint on the island: Corinthians, Byzantines, Venetians, French, Germans, and, of course, the English.

While the Durrells may have sparked my initial interest in Corfu, they weren't the only notable Brits to fall for the seductive island. There was Princess Alice, the great granddaughter of Queen Victoria and Prince Philip's mother.

Before I left on my trip, I asked my twelve-year-old grand-daughter, Sophia, who is a bit of an Anglophile, if she knew anything about the princess.

"Only that she was crazy," she answered, twirling tiny circles next to her head with her finger in the universal gesture for insanity.

"Well, some people do think that," I countered. "Only because she said God spoke to her."

"Uh-huh," my granddaughter replied. "That's something a crazy person would say."

"So do you think St. Joan of Arc was crazy? Because God spoke to her, too."

"Joan of Arc is a *saint*?"

So much for seven years of Catholic schooling.

At this point, my granddaughter was backing out of the room. Before she could escape, I had to defend this misunderstood and mostly forgotten princess. I recited an abridged version of Alice's life. She was born deaf. Despite this challenge, she did what princesses were fated to do: secure a royal match and produce heirs. She married Prince Andrew of Greece and Denmark and adopted his Greek homeland when she was eighteen. In addition to the future prince consort to Queen Elizabeth, she gave birth to four older daughters. But she was so much more than a royal baby machine.

Despite her big family, she embraced charity work, contributing to a school for impoverished girls and working in soup kitchens. When Nazis occupied Greece, Alice hid a Jewish family in her Athens home. After the war, she founded a religious order of nuns.

"Hmmm. Interesting," my granddaughter said at the conclusion of my lecture.

"Interesting" is what twelve-year-olds say when they mean the exact opposite. I couldn't blame her for her skepticism. Sane people do not hear voices, celestial or otherwise. Princesses do not become nuns. Nevertheless, Mon Repos, Alice's home on Corfu, remained on my high-priority visitation list.

I set aside my first day on the island for exploring the town of Corfu. A desk clerk at my hotel advised that if I stood in front of the neighborhood bakery, a bus would stop and take me into town. So every morning, I crowded onto the bus with the mob of Corfiots on their way to work. In the late afternoon, I joined the commute home, the passengers loaded up with a day of work worries, grocery bags, and on one occasion, a five-gallon, potted ficus tree that ended

81

up wedged against my knees. It was through these bus excursions that I came to appreciate the melting-pot nature of Corfu and to understand that everything authentic about the island came from someplace else. Consider the ubiquitous kumquat.

Groceries and specialty shops throughout the island sell kumquat products, everything from marmalade and candy to a bright orange liqueur with a twenty percent alcohol content. The family-owned Mavromatis Distillery is the most prominent purveyor of these products. At one of their shops, I stocked up on liqueur packaged in tiny glass bottles shaped like the island, thinking I had authentic Corfu souvenirs. That was before I knew about Sidney Merlin, a British botanist who introduced kumquats to Corfu sometime in the 1920s. The Brits are also credited with introducing ginger beer to the island, along with cricket.

I pondered these British legacies one afternoon while taking a snack break from shopping at Marks & Spencer. The bread and cheese I ordered at an outdoor cafe turned out to be a grilled cheese sandwich, undoubtedly another contribution of British imperialism, but satisfying in the way fried cheese can be. *Maybe authentic is overrated,* I thought.

I paid my bill and strolled toward the waterfront to visit the Old Fortress, built by the Venetians in the fifteenth century and occupied by the British in the ninteenth. Towering over a rocky peninsula at the eastern edge of town and protected by a moat, the fortress repelled the Ottomans during the nearly four centuries of Venetian rule. A walk around the fortress compound reveals a time capsule of Corfu history. A Byzantine settlement once stood there. A small museum in the gatehouse pays tribute to that heritage with fragments of religious frescoes.

The Venetian prison remains intact, but most of the surviving buildings are from the British era, now occupied by the city archives and library and the Ionian University music department. I heard cello music drifting from the old British garrison as I walked the perimeter of the battlements. I marveled at the way Corfu has reclaimed what its occupiers left behind.

This is most evident at St. George Church, overlooking the Garitsa Bay side of the fortress. Built as an Anglican church for the soldiers stationed at the fortress, the building resembles an ancient Greek temple. In 1864, when the British left and Corfu became part of Greece, the church became Greek Orthodox. Yet they kept the name of the dragon-slaying patron saint of England.

A shrine to St. George inside the entrance to the church drips with tokens left by visitors: prayer beads, small silver icons, jewelry, even a wristwatch. The church lady on duty the afternoon of my visit said people leave offerings to thank the saint for answering a prayer.

"But a wristwatch?" I questioned.

"Yes, people leave bracelets, earrings," the church lady said. "You can leave an eye to ask St. George to keep an eye on you."

By eye she meant the blue and white ceramic charms sold all over Greece to ward off evil curses. I chuckled over this decidedly Greek interpretation of how to honor a British saint.

On my last day in Corfu, I made a pilgrimage to Mon Repos. As far as royal dwellings go, the house is modest, especially for someone like Princess Alice, who was born in Windsor Castle and spent many childhood days in Buckingham Palace. The sweeping sea views, endless blue skies and the tranquil surrounding forest more than made up for the simplicity of Mon Repos. Alice must have, indeed, felt like a storybook princess when she first came to the hilltop refuge. By all accounts, she married Prince Andrew for love, and her early days in Greece were happy ones, especially during family sojourns at Mon Repos. The house itself was closed on the day I visited, and the surrounding parkland was nearly deserted. I met only a few joggers and dog walkers on the dirt paths, affording me a quiet space to reflect on the mysterious princess I'd come to pay my respects to.

Time and again, tragedy infiltrated her life. During the Russian revolution, Bolsheviks slaughtered her favorite aunt, Ella, sister to Czarina Alexandra and founder of a convent in Russia. Her aunt's murder inspired a feverish religious devotion, which Alice's biographer, Hugo Vickers, judged a major factor in the breakdown of Alice's marriage. He gives less credit to her husband's womanizing.

When the Greeks ousted the royal family in 1922, Alice was set adrift with her children, never again to call Mon Repos her home. Although they didn't divorce, her prince lived out his life in the south of France with a mistress, while Alice struggled. At one point, her family carted Alice off, against her will, to a Swiss asylum. They kept her there for nearly three years. I can't help but wonder if this was out of concern for Alice's mental health or to save themselves embarrassment.

Eventually Alice returned to Greece, where she continued charity work, most notably the hiding of a Jewish family from the Nazis. For that act she has the status of Righteous Among the Nations, an honor Israel awards to those who risked their lives to save Jews during the Holocaust.

It was after WWII that Alice attempted to found a religious order of nuns, as her Aunt Ella had done in Russia. Alice never took vows, and the convent never quite succeeded. Still, for the rest of her life she dressed in a grey habit, even after Prince Phillip and Queen Elizabeth convinced her to leave Greece to live in Buckingham Palace. She died there and, according to her wishes, is buried in Jerusalem.

Amid all the heartache, at least Alice had happy memories of those early days on Corfu.

I left Mon Repos comforted with those thoughts. It was the sunniest and bluest of days. Shunning the bus, I walked back into town along the water. When I reached old town Corfu, I encountered bronze relief sculptures of the two famous Durrell writers, Lawrence and his youngest brother, Gerald, on whose memoirs the TV series is based. They are immortalized, not as the young man and child they were when they first came to Corfu, but as old men, wrinkled, portly, exuding the successes launched by their sojourn on this magical island.

The inscription on the base of Lawrence Durrell's sculpture reads, "Greece is the country that offers you the discovery of yourself."

I think that was especially true for Princess Alice and maybe a little bit for me. Certainly my concept of *authentic* changed. The people of Corfu wove authenticity from the threads of many cultures, embracing what was good, changing what invaders left behind into something fit for an island paradise.

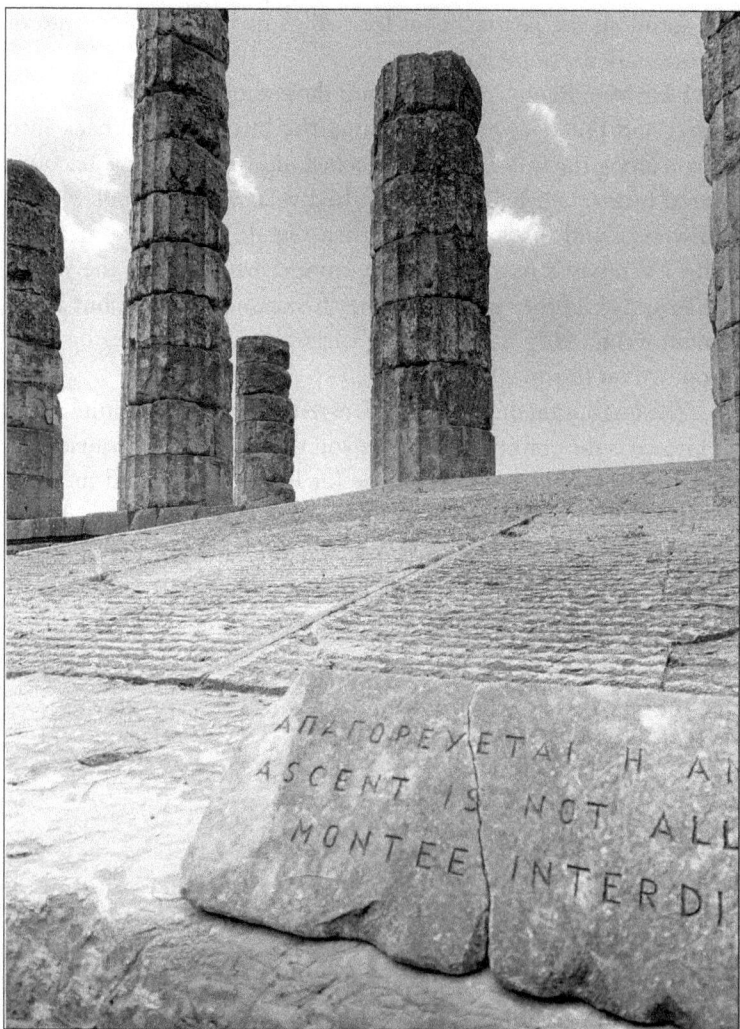

The ruins at Delphi on Mount Parnassus

HIGH ON MOUNT PARNASSUS

Tom Harrell

The future is a tricky thing. By definition just out of reach, it teases us with the thought that IF we could just take a peek behind the curtain, could only know what lay in store a month, a day, an hour, even seconds ahead, we would be ... divine, if not quite immortal.

The ancients thought it possible, if inspired by the gods, to see the future. The Oracle of Delphi was famous in the ancient world for her prophecies of the future, ambiguous though they might be. Later, "science" told us it was impossible to know the future and the Oracle, if she made inspired predictions at all, might simply have been high on fumes. Nowadays, theoretical physics and "The Big Bang Theory" teach us there might be an infinite number of universes, and therefore infinite futures. Predicting "the" future suddenly seems so ... ancient.

I considered this, along with my sanity, as I climbed the steep slope of Mount Parnassus to see what remains of the Delphi ruins. The summer sun beat down on the throngs, a mix of tourists and guides hiking, resting, explaining, complaining and, of course, taking selfies. The slight breeze did not whisper prophecy. The weathered stones were silent too; their secrets are not to be shared.

Had the Oracle seen this future? Of decline and ruin and loss of faith, the Olympian gods and goddesses fading to myth as one god replaced the many? Of tourists eager to find just the right photo op, resting their large bottoms where once she moved kingdoms?

Or had she seen, those many years ago, that the future was not one event but infinite possibilities more numerous than the stars in the sky? Perhaps that is why the Oracle's predictions were famously opaque.

Or maybe, frustrated by impatient Greeks and bossy priests, forever growing rich on her labor, she simply slipped away one hot afternoon much like the one we endured, her face covered for shade, no one the wiser. Maybe she saw a better future in the next valley, or at the ends of the Earth. Maybe she saw many possible futures and left to live them all.

All we know, for certain, is that Delphi now lies in ruins. And even if it did not, we are too cynical, too wed to algorithms and codes, now conditioned to ask Google, itself the modern Oracle, to tell us what to believe. A new god has risen, created by man. You really cannot blame a girl for leaving.

In fact, the Oracle was not a single immortal woman, but a long series of priestesses chosen for their ability to serve as a portal to the divine words of Apollo. Known as the "Pythia," this woman could shape events within Greece and beyond, though humble farmers and artisans also could seek her insight.

But I asked myself: How did the Pythia prophesize the future? As a fan of Greek history and myth—my first real book was an illustrated compilation of Greek myths—the Oracle was a source of endless fascination. Just how did she do it, and just how could I get in on this? Or was I a couple of millennia too late?

The one and only answer given by her contemporaries for her

divine insight was religious. Life in ancient Greece was inextricably bound in ritual and sacrifice. The gods were capricious beings and did not hesitate to interfere in human affairs. No significant decision was made—from pursuing war to planting wheat—without first seeking the blessing of the gods. And what better way to determine the gods' will than to consult directly with them? Enter the oracles.

Contemplating these questions as I struggled up the mountain, I reviewed what I knew of the Pythia's origins. According to legend, Zeus released two golden eagles, one to fly east, the other west, and they met at Delphi, the center of the Earth. It was here the infant god Apollo vanquished the giant python of Gaia, casting its body into the chasm below. The fumes of the rotting python rose through the chasm to inspire divine insight. The high priestess became known as the Pythia, and by the seventh century BCE the cult of Apollo was well established as the sanctuary grew in size and prominence. It would flourish for centuries.

Though the Pythia was the most influential woman in ancient Greece, her rise was not an ode to feminism. When too many men died inhaling the fumes, it was decided a woman, preferably a beautiful young virgin, of course, should become the sacred portal. But given the predilection of men to seduce (or kidnap) the young and lovely Pythia, the role later was reserved for women over fifty, though they were dressed as virgins. (Apparently, fifty was not considered the new forty). The Pythia certainly was the most famous and respected of the oracles, but she was not alone. Others, too, were said to speak for Apollo and even Zeus himself. How, then, to choose?

One legend has it that Croesus, King of Lydia in modern Turkey, sought to test the oracles by sending messengers to seven of the most prominent oracles of the Mediterranean world and simultaneously asking each this question: What was the king doing that day? Setting aside the logistical improbability of this exercise, the Oracle of Delphi was declared the winner. The Pythia's remarkable answer: "I count the grains of the sand on the beach and measure the sea; I understand the speech of the dumb and hear the voiceless. The smell has come to my senses of a … tortoise boiling and bubbling with a lamb's flesh…."

Apparently, the king was indeed enjoying a lunch of tortoise and lamb stew.

So how did she know the future, or claim to? Was she in fact a portal for Apollo as the ancients believed? Was her link to Apollo aided by sacred fumes or the prophetic waters of the nearby spring? The historian Claudian claimed that when Apollo returned each year to Delphi, "the sacred ripple revisits the surface of the waters, a clear echo resounds from the shrine, and the now-inspired rocks tremble to the voice of prophecy."

Modern speculation is far less poetic. Explanations range from the geologic—volatile gas fumes such as ethylene rose from the rocks below the temple (and not, apparently, from the carcass of a giant python) and permeated the small room where the Pythia sat, inducing hallucinations; to the toxicological—the Pythia chewed oleander leaves or inhaled the smoke of burning oleander, again inducing hallucinations; to the cynical—the Pythia and her priests simply shaped the answers to fit the politics of the moment; to the slightly less cynical—the Pythia and/or her priests deliberately gave ambiguous predictions so no matter what happened they could claim to be right (and keep the donations flowing).

No one, at least no one seeking tenure, seems to entertain the idea that she indeed heard directly from Apollo.

The ancient Greeks had no such doubts. Kings and commoners alike traveled to Delphi to seek her wisdom. It must be said, though, that a famous name or hefty donation moved one quickly up the line. Some things never change. The Pythia heard questions—carefully vetted by her priests—only on the seventh day of every month, a day holy to Apollo, and only during nine months of the year because Apollo—no fool—left Mount Parnassus during the coldest three months for warmer climes.

Whether the Pythia's prophecies were spoken directly by her to the supplicant or were instead "interpreted" by her priests (in dactylic hexameter no less) is not known. Nor is it known if her predictions were spoken plainly or were delivered like divine but ambiguous fortune cookies, though some five hundred prophecies attributed to the Pythia survive. An opportunity for a best-selling book, perhaps?

I thought to myself, what would I have asked the Pythia? If given one chance to tap the wisdom of a god? Ideas crowded my imagination: How long to do I have? Does true love lie ahead? Or less selfishly, is peace possible? And how is it achieved?

Perhaps modern life affords us the luxury of navel-gazing. I felt overwhelmed by the fear of "wasting" my question. Even now, I wrestle with what I would ask. In contrast, the ancient world had more practical concerns: Kings asked the best time for war, farmers the best time to sow crops. Life was immediate and pressing.

What would you ask the Oracle?

The Pythia reached the pinnacle of her prestige around the fifth century BCE. Confronted by the vast Persian army about this time, Athens beseeched the Oracle for advice. Should they fight? Flee?

Her famous prophecy said only that "a wall of wood alone shall be uncaptured." The Athenians could not agree on the meaning:

Did she mean build a wooden palisade around the Acropolis? Take to their ships, abandon Athens, and rebuild in Italy? Or, as urged by Themistocles, battle the Persians with the Athenian Navy?

In the end, all three ideas were adopted: A palisade was built, some Athenians fled, and though Athens was burned to the ground, the Athenian Navy defeated the larger Persian fleet at Salamis. It seems the Pythia was right ... though fleeing to Italy might also have worked and fulfilled the prophecy as well.

If an Oracle can mean several things, does it mean anything? Standing in the wilting heat, I felt vaguely disappointed as I surveyed the fallen stones. I wanted a straightforward answer to my precious question—if I could ever land on it—not mystery, even if wrapped in poetry.

And I am not alone. It is said that when the Pythia refused to give a prophecy to Alexander the Great, he dragged her by the hair from her chamber until she cried, "You are invincible, boy!" To which he replied, "Now I have my answer."

Perhaps he had climbed these very steps in the same heat.

Much later, the emperor Nero, angered by the Pythia's dismissal of his question, had her burned alive. The gradual decline of Olympian worship and rise of Christianity proved greater threats than impatient conquerors or insane emperors. Conquered by Rome, the Greek gods had been adopted—one might say appropriated—by the victors. Christianity increasingly displaced "pagan" worship throughout the empire. By the fourth century CE, the Oracle was in serious decline, and some argue the Temple of Apollo was already in ruins.

The last recorded prophecy was the Pythia's most poignant. Approached by Rome's last pagan emperor, Julian the Apostate, who sought to re-establish the oracles, the Pythia is said to have lamented: "Tell the emperor that the Daidalic hall has fallen. No longer does Phoebus have his chamber, nor mantic laurel, nor prophetic spring; and the speaking water has been silenced."

This last prophecy was not ambiguous. It was simply heartbreaking. Maybe, I thought, straightforward is not always best.

Though sometimes attributed to later Christian opponents of paganism, the last prophecy was, according to one scholar, unquestionably a "sad and moving expression of the passing of an old order of things" and its elegant hexameter the "last fragment of Greek poetry which has moved the hearts of men" for a thousand years.

The ruins of the Oracle also made me sad. I'm not sure why, or even what I expected. To have my future predicted? To feel some divine inspiration, some hint of the sacred? But nothing like that stirred in me on that hot, dusty hillside. It seemed abandoned, in every sense.

In my childhood, reading the Greek myths, it seemed so easy: Ask, and you will be answered. The question, or even the answer, seemed less important than the wonder of a divine portal. But the unquestioning faith that sustained the Oracle for a millennium is gone. Monotheism and its historic frenemy, science, have combined to relegate the Greek gods—and their chosen spokeswomen—to polite intellectual inquiry or even myth.

The Pythia famously named Socrates as the wisest man in the world. Socrates replied that if this was so, it was only because he alone was aware of his ignorance, and so he pursued a life of learning. Like Socrates and the other giants of philosophy and art, the stellar minds of classical Greece saw no contradiction between intellect and the divine. Indeed, one was a gift from the other. Their faith, like fuel, sustained the oracles.

You cannot manufacture faith, and sadly, a man raised in a mono-secular-humanistic-science-theistic culture will never hear the "lustrous voice" of an oracle, as Homer so described it. If faith fueled the Oracle, it is no surprise her voice has fallen silent.

But I have not given up hope. The Pythia is out there, somewhere. I sometimes imagine I see her as I run errands around Phoenix, a fifty-something retiree dressed in a crisp white skirt and matching blouse, with a mean golf game and a suspiciously handsome young caddy, a Greek god, so to speak, enjoying the Arizona sun for three months a year.

Maybe she is restless and ready to resume her role. And around my house are plenty of oleander bushes.

Euboean lekythos (vase for oil) with a representation of a lion,
535 – 525 BCE

LIONS IN MY PAST

Sandra Bracken

I. Delos

I step onto the weedy terrace,
looking up, not down, looking
at the lions frozen, attentive,
ribs visible, stretched beyond real.

Each next to the other, lined up
like soldiers facing one direction: east;
ready, protective,
jaws agape in defiance of history,

reminders of gentle Leto, a goddess
desperate to find a safe place to give birth
and Delos became that sacred setting.
How many lions bore witness to

the birth of Apollo and twin sister Artemis
under the single palm tree?

A miracle on that tiny ragged island
so many eons ago.

The stately lions roar in silence,
perhaps in celebration, in triumph;
perhaps protesting the ravages of time
rendering their weatherworn stone
meaningless.

II. Mycenae

I wander until no more,
the pebbly path too long in the midday sun.
In the shade of the cyclopian stone wall, I sit,
sense the majesty of a place that was.

Taking out my sketchpad and pencil I begin.
(A drawing is an intimate recording of time and place.)
Two lionesses, symbols of power, carved in stone
rise above the entrance to the citadel.

Poised, facing each other,
their strength visible in thigh and shoulder
muscles supporting the standing pose.
Their forepaws rest on an altar between them.

It is obvious to wonder
what happened to their heads.
(A drawing is an intimate recording of time and place.)

It is obvious to wonder
who passed below en route to the Mycenaean capital.

Oh, the stories you would tell but cannot:
proud Agamemnon coming home from war
returning to his wife Clytemnestra and his death.
No doubt brave Orestes traveled through your gate

and sad Cassandra who could see the future
   in ruins—the odyssey of ancient times
(A drawing is an intimate recording of time and place)

The story today is of curious crowds and eager visitors
and one absorbed in silent images.

Zorba the Greek Ballet in Maribor, 2008

Zorba or Epicurus

Gayle McGill

Zorba or Epicurus? Which will animate this trip to Greece. Forty years ago, when I first traveled to Greece, I read *Zorba the Greek* and delighted in his passion and philosophies and descriptions of the land. On that trip, my husband and I stumbled upon a magical Zorba-like experience that lives as bright in my mind today as the sun shining on the Ionian Sea did then.

We were young, spunky and a little feral. Married just a year, we were on summer break after our first year of teaching. Our travel style was seat-of-the-pants. Nothing planned. Everything possible. Including wasting endless days trying to get from one place to another in the cheapest possible manner and never knowing where we'd sleep that night except that it would be inexpensive and probably funky.

Our magical Greek experience started out anything but. After days bumbling around Athens in immense heat, our backpacks heavy we decided a ferry to Corfu was the answer.

There we stood on the pier the ticket agent had noted and watched a huge ferry leave the adjacent dock. It finally sunk in. THAT was the twice-a-week ferry to Corfu. We wanted to jump into the sea and swim after it but instead walked back to town, snapping at each other, our spirits low.

Three days later we stepped off the ferry at Corfu Town. We found a tiny second-floor room out of town, whitewashed and spare, with a large window facing the water. Happiness flooded through me each time I opened those shutters to the shimmering sea. At night I lay in bed reading *Zorba the Greek* while the moonlight rippled across the water, always attentive to the many sounds of the sea.

The whole scene was as far as you could get from the cold gunmetal-gray lakes rimmed with dense buggy green that I'd grown up with in Ontario. Not that I didn't love that scape, but it was a place were a ditch was considered geography, warm sunny days were few, and a dour Presbyterianism ruled the land.

Corfu was different. Corfu was sea and rocky shore with beautiful cliffs and sunny days galore. Corfu was lovely villages with yummy cheap food and drink and music too. There were enchanting Greek myths to consider, filled with naughty gods and history written in poetry. Corfu was the most wonderful place I had ever been.

The days passed, then the weeks. We rowed out on the sea as far as our arms could take us and swam and explored nearby coves. Our bodies turned brown, our hearts thawed and opened wide. I knew I was the most alive and beautiful that I would ever be. I felt part Zorba surging with passionate appetites, part Gaia mother goddess connected to the land with my strength coming from the brilliant light. There was only one thing to do. I must stay, even if it was alone. I belonged in this landscape.

Zorba goaded me on. "Let your youth have free reign; it won't come again, so be bold and no repenting."

Perhaps, I'd be a shepherdess nimbly climbing up the steep cliffs to idyllic pastures. Nah. Too much excrement. Maybe a schoolteacher. I'd have to learn Greek anyway. I pictured myself as an old woman sitting on a rough porch in a little house high on a cliff. I imagined scrambling over the rocks to visit other old women like myself. We'd gossip and talk of the sea. And on and on my mind churned searching for an escape from the long gray winters of home.

We did leave the Canadian winters behind and moved to California. I've not lived the life of a shepherdess or even schoolteacher for long. I've had a challenging but exciting career as a programmer, wife and mother.

Now, I look down at my old lady hands as I pack my suitcase on my way to Greece again. Could Greece rekindle my old dreams? Dean Burnett, author of *Idiot Brain* tells us that the context in which we acquire episodic memories is all-important. If we are again in that context those times may come flooding back like Proust's *madeleine* moment. How I longed to feel the passionate senses of youth again. Just for a day. Just for an hour. Feel that pull of rock and sea and sun. Could it happen? Could I manage to get myself back into the almost ecstatic state of my first trip?

I tried rereading *Zorba*. The character felt dated and paternalistic. I turned to *Travels with Epicurus* by Daniel Klein. In it, Daniel visits Hydra and spends time among the local culture and searches Epicurus's writings for clues on how to have the best possible life as an old person. Given that this is what I am now—an old person––I'm all ears.

According to Epicurus, I probably already know the answer. "It is not the young man who should be considered fortunate but the old man who has lived well, because the young man in his prime wanders much by chance, vacillating in his beliefs, while the old man has docked in the harbor, having safeguarded his true happiness."

So back to Greece we went with our TSA Pre-Check, well-thumbed guidebooks, pre-booked accommodation and each day meticulously planned. Of course, this being Greece, the plans went off the rails immediately, starting with our taxi driver getting hopelessly lost trying to find our perfectly findable Airbnb in Athens. Then there was the heat: each day a dance with heat stroke, the crowds sometimes overwhelming.

Athens was hard work, but oh, the wondrous museums, the spectacle of the Evzone and the joy of walking the maze of streets around the Acropolis and through the Zappeion Gardens. We poked through every ruin, saw an opera in the Odeon Herodes Atticus, toured the mainland sites of Mycenae, Olympia and the jewel of them all, Delphi.

We were ready this time. We had knowledge and perspective. We gobbled up each experience with glee. We also gobbled up the finest food and drink we could find and stayed in wonderful Airbnb's in lively neighborhoods.

I did not feel young or passionate or beautiful for even a moment. Mostly just wicked hot. The light and sea still pulled. I was deeply moved by the beauty of Delphi. This time we did not endlessly bicker. We've learned how to travel together in kindness. There were no wasted days like long ago. We had more respect and perspective this time for what Greece has given the world and the strength of the Greek people. It was a pleasant trip all in all and the definition of a safe-harbor experience.

Is transformative travel, like my youth, a thing of the past? No way. I'm back home again packing for my next trip to Crescent City in northern California. I plan to hike every redwood grove I can and kayak every river that I'm able to. Will this trip be full of excitement and surprises? I bet yes. Passion. Yes, again. Has the trip been meticulously planned? Absolutely. Zorba and Epicurus. Age has delivered me both.

The author's Greek garden, post-oxalis

In My Greek Garden I am God

Annelize Goedbloed

Weeding. A recurrent job in springtime. I don't like it at all. It is like vacuum cleaning outdoors. But I do I have this house on the island of Paros and that means upkeep. After all, I think it is best to have friends with property; you visit them, praise them for the beauty of it and leave the upkeep to them. But here I am.

Almost rhythmically I pull the weeds.

A bee swaying in the soft breeze as if in a hammock is filling the air with its hum. The heavy lime soil is soft and sticky. People say it has rained an awful lot this winter in the last fifteen years. I can see that; weeds and weeds. Especially oxalis.

Oxalis pes-caprae, false shamrocks, wood sorrel, Bermuda buttercup. Whatever its name, I hate it. It is growing like a carpet, obscuring and smothering all other plants. They even have the guts to produce quite attractive yellow flowers that make me feel guilty in my systematic attack.

Wikipedia informs me: "Characteristic of many members of this genus is that they contain oxalic acid (whose name references the genus), giving the leaves and flowers a sour taste, refreshing to chew in small amounts. However, in large amounts these species are toxic, interfering with proper digestion and kidney function."

I knew it. Already without eating them, I feel the indigestion and kidney problems coming on. Even in this soft soil the Oxalis resist furiously to my pulling its roots out together with its long, elastic stems. Later in the year, when we'll have several dry, hot summer months in this Mediterranean climate, they will wither into a fragile brown crust that will lie over all the plants they now hide with a green blanket of their clover-like leaves. But by then they will have triumphed already with the multiplication of many more bulblets.

I carefully move my little blue Ikea stool to another strategic place to tackle the next square meter. Its thick blunt legs prevent me from sinking into the muddier places. It is comfortable not to have to be on your knees and bend and get up all the time. I brush the weeds forward, exposing their stems, pull them out, roll them up and throw them, tangled into a ball, toward the waiting wheelbarrow. A neat system, I think.

In the garden I am God. It is I who decide what is allowed to grow and what not. That is why I can't have a gardener. He might take out wild plants that I allow to stay. The little curry-smelling flowers for example. The consequence is that I can't get up straight in the morning, my back stiff and aching from being bent over hours and hours, fanatically pulling, hacking and wheel-barrowing.

It is Me who is the All Mighty now. If I want a garden of man-high thistles, wonderful. If I want a garden of mean stinging nettles, so what.

But oxalis. No. I have declared war on this plant.

Indigenous to South Africa, *oxalis pes-caprae* is a highly invasive, noxious weed in many parts of the world. It was all the mistake of one curator of the botanical garden of Malta who brought this plant from its native country to Malta in 1806. In a few years it was found outside the garden, and in the following years it spread. To Italy, Greece, the whole Mediterranean, via the Middle East it arrived in India and it reached Australia, and in the other direction, Northern Africa, and from Portugal to the Southern parts of England and the United States and Central America and further down pushing out native plant species for light and space, and also working to inhibit the germination of native species. I read that it was fortunate that this curator had a sterile type of plant so it will never have fruits and seeds. It apparently makes little bulblets on the lower part of the stem and on the roots, each bulblet capable of producing more than twenty bulblets per year. So it spreads quickly if someone moves or removes the plant or the ground where it grows. New plants mature rapidly, and then it spreads like a plague. Can you imagine if it would also spread from seeds!

My hand with the torn glove—I do try to keep my hands ladylike—approaches the stems of the plants that I have doomed. I wonder, *Can they feel the menace?* Like we humans feel when a snake slithers forward to attack? Ever more precise and refined instruments and chemical analyses show that plants react to the gnawing of caterpillars. Otherwise they seem harmless and defenseless creatures, sitting there fixed in soil and rock, not capable of running away from danger. Some try something mean with spines, stingers or poisonous saps, but the poor things are mostly left to the Grace of God. Or a self-declared god like me now in my garden.

Every now and then I feel almost guilty. That dandelion, do I leave it? Its flower shines radiant like a little sun and looks up at me innocently. Its tender spring leaves would make a nice salad, but I don't feel like a dandelion salad today, so the dice fall and out it goes. It resists, ferociously holding onto the earth with its long firm root. A flock of seagulls flutters across the sun, calling out happily when they catch a wind to surf.

The abundance of oxalis, its tyranny in my garden, has made me belligerent. I wonder, *What is the purpose of its creation?* There are in fact a great many creations of the All Mighty of which I don't understand the purpose. If these are meant to release anger, there might be a purpose. We need anger to relieve ourselves. Anger is like a karate growl that liberates energy. It is quite different from another kind of anger that makes us angry because it debilitates us and sucks us dry, the self-destructive anger, the anger that degrades us. Pulling the weeds, I am enjoying my anger, my awful thoughts about useless creations.

A little black cap starts twittering nervously in the nearby bush, piercing the silence, when I get up to put my stool a bit forward. How can I make it clear that this god-in-the-garden is no threat to birds, that I am a lower god and only allowed a limited array of death certificates. The general concept of life and death is not mine. It was conceived by the All Mighty. I think it was a good concept for us humans because who really, seriously, wants to be immortal. It must be boring to know that time doesn't matter, that nothing can be missed because there is always time to do it, that nothing can be regretted because there is always time to make up for it. For plants and animals there are probably other considerations if only because they are much less in control of their lives than humans. I don't think boredom is among their worries, but I can't be sure. The little black cap should worry now about that wild cat that I chased away when I came out for my gardening.

I bend back a cluster of the delicate heads of oxalis, exposing their pale stems. They resemble human sinews in the way human can mean frailty and endurance both at the same time. The little tug with which I sever them from the soil generates a very small snapping sound. Would they feel it like the snap of a breaking limb?

I fill up the wheelbarrow with the plant corpses. A thistle gives me a reproachful sting.

With a straight back and head held high I carry the load to the stake, the place of the Last Judgement.

I look at my garden, satisfied with my job, satisfied with my selection of the weeds I left.

I can almost hear their whispers of *thank you, thank you* when I pass.

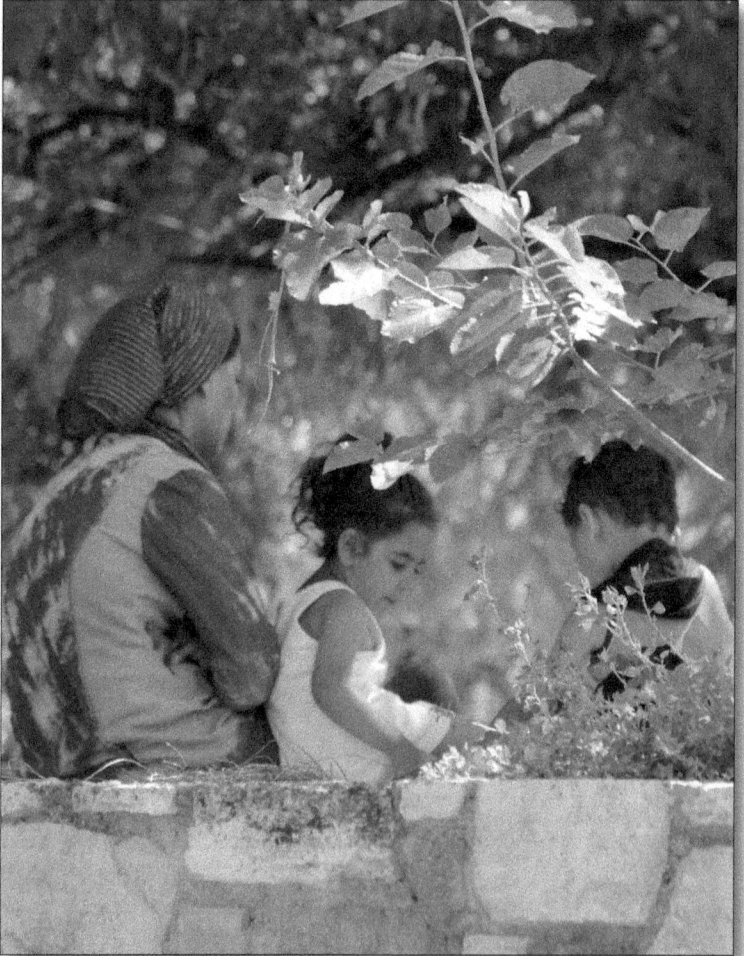

Refugee family rests in shade on island of Kos

Travelers and Gifts

Joanna Biggar

Alighting from the ferry to Kos after a short passage from Bodrum, Turkey, we found not the idyllic holiday island we imagined, but Greece in crisis. There was an economic crisis—the banks had recently closed, causing great hardship; and a humanitarian crisis— thousands of refugees had overwhelmed the country. Many of them, like us, had landed on the island of Kos. Women in long dresses and head scarves, fatigued and grizzled men in battered shirts, and children surrounded us. Hundreds of children roamed the streets, many in rags and barefoot, many appearing to belong to no one. We had read of the economic woes, and the flotillas of refugees—most from Syria—landing on Greek shores, who had made the desperate crossing from Turkey on small, leaky boats or rafts to reach the safe-haven of asylum in Europe. But stepping into this maelstrom, we experienced what news reports cannot convey.

My husband Doug, our family, and I made that trip from Bodrum on a hot July day in 2015. We had come to vacation in Turkey with my daughter Heather, her husband Kevin, and their three children who had been living many years in Indonesia. In honor of the doctors in our family, we decided to visit Kos, the birthplace of Hippocrates, make a pilgrimage to a healing temple of Asclepius, enjoy the sights, and to eat ice cream.

Two months after our shock upon landing, a photo of a dead Syrian boy, three-year-old Alan Kurdi, who had washed ashore near Bodrum, went viral. His overcrowded boat had capsized. The image of the child, who looked to be peacefully napping, brought the essence of the disaster we had entered to conscience of the world.

Now it is June 2019, four years later. I have returned to Greece to teach, and am still trying to make sense of what we found on Kos. I have thought a lot about the short crossing we made, starting from the same place near Bodrum where Alan Kurdi was found. I note, too, that I use prevailing label—refugees—when speaking of those fleeing poverty, war, death. They, however, must see themselves differently: as asylum seekers, survivors, human beings following the basic human impulse to migrate in order to find a better life. Yet others choose what to name them. And when their numbers swell, they are by turns called migrants, illegals, invaders, swarms, hordes.

I, too, am a seeker. When people like me show up in great numbers, we may be also called invaders—or missionaries, occupiers, tourists. But we are free to come and go. So we label ourselves with a name that reflects the advantages of those with choices: travelers. Somewhere in this tangle of terms, of privileges, I want to find what seems lost—the thread of our common humanity.

The heat continued to rise as the day progressed on the island of Kos. We left aside thoughts of magnificent ruins and magical beaches to find our way to the bus which climbed to Asclepius' temple, feeling overcome in the midst of crowds we were now part of. The bus stop was near a small park churning with kids, and the wait long. My grandchildren were happy to enter, to join in play with other children, and reluctant to leave when the bus finally arrived. But we boarded, noting that the small fare was out of the reach of those around us. Climbing up a shaded road, we soon reached the gates and towering columns of the ancient site.

There is a picture commemorating that day on our fridge. We are seated against an old wall, having clambered through the ruins and learned all the guidebooks could tell us of Hippocrates' teachings, of the importance of rituals, medicine, religion and spas. In the background, there are no refugees. We have escaped them.

I am not proud to say this. In fact, I am ashamed. But caught up in the enormity of the situation, the tragedy of it, in the moment I could think of no positive way to respond.

Luckily, that was not the case for my daughter, who the year before, along with her friend Ashley, had confronted the same crush of immigrants arriving in Jakarta. Most of them were also from the Middle East—from Iran, Afghanistan, Pakistan, and some from Iraq and Syria. They had come seeking asylum in Australia, and found themselves like the immigrants on Kos would be, when the border closed, stuck in place. One day my daughter said to her friend, "Someone ought to do something."

"That's when," she said, "I realized that someone was us."

So in 2014, the two women overcame the obstacles of prejudice, xenophobia, sexism, religious intolerance (many of the newly arrived were Christian) and found the means, the staff (volunteer), and the place—a private house that needed renovation. There, they opened a school, which also serves as a de facto refugee center. The community chose the name, The Roshan Learning Center, Roshan meaning bright in Farsi.

In the years since, I have visited Roshan many times and met its participants, many of them Afghans, at social events or at my daughter's airy home with lush gardens, where they were guests, and sometimes residents. In my photo album, there is a picture of me surrounded by women wrapped in beautiful scarves, capturing a moment when we shared stories about grandchildren.

Back in Greece, those other refugees on the other side of the world come to mind as I picture them, see their faces, remember their names. I know, of course, that the problem of thousands—millions—of people on the move, uprooted from their homes because of political, economic or climate disasters, is a global one. In my own country it is a daily horror to see the treatment of honest, desperate people seeking the basics of a decent life coming to our borders to be treated like criminals, thrown into detention centers, with children ripped from parents, and toddlers and infants put in cages. The president maintains that the ultimate way to stop this "invasion" is to build a wall.

I wonder, now, four years after I first encountered it here, how the continuing problem is being addressed in Greece. So I seek some experts to find out.

In the offices of the International Refugee Committee in downtown Athens, I sit down with two dedicated and very capable young women, Anastasia Gavrili and Eftychia Zeorziadi, who fill me in on the basics: There are about 76,000 migrants in Greece, 3,800 to 4,000 of them unaccompanied minors. Eftychia, who works in child services, says most of those are boys above 14. But some are girls, and they are immediately put in safe places.

At the beginning of the crisis, in 2015, migrants could traverse Greece to enter other E.U. countries. In those days, Anastasia explains, non-governmental organizations, such as IRC, handled mostly everything. But many things have changed. Most countries have slowed down their admittance of migrants, and some borders—such as the borders with Turkey—have closed. Huge bottlenecks and encampments have resulted. In Greece, for example, many islands—Lesbos, Chios, Samos, Lemnos, as well as Kos—are now de facto migrant camps. The Greek government, with a lot of financial aid from the European Union, has taken over the retention of refugees. But, Anastasia stresses, the NGOs, which are very experienced and can move swiftly, are still in fact very involved.

Those who attain prized refugee status are provided with certain basic supports. There are camps in Athens, for example, where official refugees are housed. But, she explains, those trapped on the islands are in deplorable conditions and wait endlessly for their status to be determined. The situation can lead to mental crises. "A lot of funding has come to Greece," she says, "a lot of help. But keeping people in that condition [for so long] is to send a political message: We're full."

I leave with new information, the names of some refugee camps in Athens, and an understanding: Even when people of good intent try to make whole cloth of our common humanity, the fabric is easily torn.

It is June and brutally hot. Before leaving our apartment in Piraeus, two things happen that fall in the realm of synchronicity, that most Greek of concepts. I receive a long note from the Roshan Center giving me a positive update on an Afghan family I befriended in Jakarta. Then a news feed points me to a story of the U.S. administration arguing in court that safe and humane treatment of children does not include giving them soap, toothbrushes, a bed. The accompanying image is of a small girl, three perhaps, lying asleep with a thumb in her mouth utterly alone on a bare linoleum floor. She has not even an aluminum blanket. I weep and shut the computer.

This is the day I will visit the Eloneas Refugee Camp near central Athens. The residents, I understand, are nearly all Afghans. Doug kindly agrees to accompany me. We leave the air-conditioned comforts and modern efficiency of the Athens metro and step into the dust and noise of an industrial zone. Trucks rumble ceaselessly past. We see fences, factories, debris and graffiti, but have no idea where the camp is. There are no signs, and if there were, we couldn't read them.

With vague instructions from a salesman, we cross dangerous roads and sidestep litter. In our camera rests a picture of a blocks-long fence with street art depicting border fences, security patrols, misery.

Doug points out it is 94 F., that we are in the direct sun, nearly out of water, and have no clear idea of where we are going. Then within minutes we see Afghan women, some with children, walking by, and I'm reminded that among refugees, these are the lucky ones. Not travelers perhaps, but they are sponsored and have support; most importantly, they can work. We find the camp entrance and understand that this is now not an NGO-sponsored facility, but one run by the Greek government. Officials wearing E.U. symbols on their vests stand at the gates. No, they tell us politely, we may not enter without an official permit from the Greek ministry, which we know could take months. No, we may not take any photographs. The image I take away is locked in my mind. Small tin houses planted in the dirt and brightly painted as if a shoreline holiday. Women in graceful dresses and headscarves, some pushing strollers. Coming and going.

Of course, on my own, I could speak to the camp's residents as they walk the street. But suddenly, I am tongue-tied. What could I possibly say? That I have met your sisters on the other side of the world? That I hope things turn out better for you? I realize I am not there to speak, but to bear witness. My unspoken message is only this: "I see you. I will remember."

We leave moved, unspeaking.

An interview I did years ago with the great Greek singer, Nana Mouskouri, upon her becoming UNICEF's Ambassador of Goodwill, comes to mind. She said it is love most of all that she must impart to the world's children, and she would deliver it through song. I, too, have love for these children, these families, yet feel bereft. I have no such gifts to impart.

I had always assumed that in the matter of gifts, of reaching across the divides that separate us one from the other, lucky from unlucky, traveler from refugee—the outreach, the understanding would come from us, the privileged. Then another scene that for four years has invaded my dreams comes to me again. I see now I have been looking in the wrong direction.

We were waiting for the bus on Kos, outside the barren playground. My grandchildren, Tatum, eight, and Clara and Finn, six, quickly jumped into the world of other children. Play, even without words, came easily, and took away the sting of dust and heat even as it erased the worlds between them. Clara soon found a little girl with darting black eyes holding a worn rag doll. Like little girls everywhere, they entered an imaginary realm with a doll as its star. And when Clara was summoned to board the bus—to escape with us—she frowned, then offered her new friend a toy bracelet. In return, the girl smiled, held out her hand and her gift, her only possession, the doll.

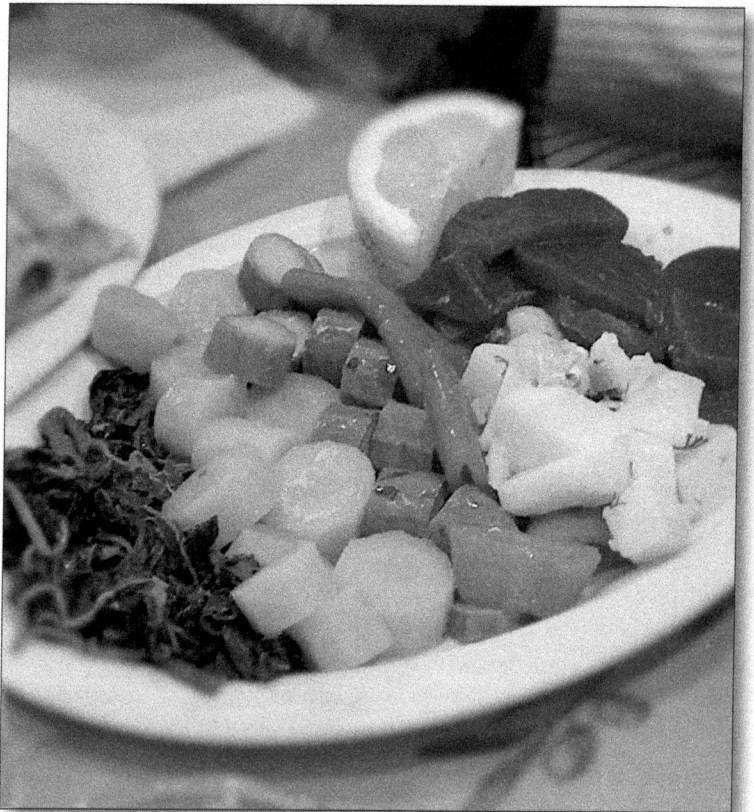

A typical Ikarian meal includes healthful vegetables

IKARIA

Sandra Bracken

"Don't go too close to the sun." I thought that a strange response after telling a friend I was going to Ikaria. What about the Greek island would prompt that remark? Then I remembered young Icarus; how his youthful enthusiasm ended in his death.

That myth begins on Crete where Icarus and his father, Daedalus, were imprisoned by King Minos. Daedalus, a master craftsman, fashioned two sets of wings made of wood, feathers and wax. They would fly to freedom. He cautioned his son that getting too close to the sun would melt the wax. Perhaps, overly excited by the effectiveness of the wings and carried away by the vision of freedom, Icarus forgot his father's warning. Flying too high, the wax melted, and his wings failed. Sadly, young Icarus fell to his death near the island that now bears his name.

Celebrating my eightieth birthday, I found myself thinking, *What's next?* Having read a book years ago entitled *The Blue Zones: Lessons for Living Longer from the People Who've Lived the Longest* by Dan Buettner, I knew that Ikaria, named for one who died too young, is one of those blue zones of longevity.

The terminology "blue zone" originated with Dr. Michael Poulain, a demographer, who drew circles in blue on a map of the planet to indicate places where people live long lives. He, Buettner and Dr. Gianni Nez, with help from the National Institute on Aging, The National Geographic Society and others, determined, after years of research, there were five such zones. I wanted to visit one where I could, first hand, get some hints on aging well. I wanted to see for myself if there's some magic elixir, some useful secret for aging well. A trip to Greece for a writing workshop presented the perfect opportunity for me to visit the island of Ikaria. However, my years of experience told me to be realistic about what I hoped to learn. Sadly young Icarus did not have the advantage of age.

As the plane from Athens approached, the island appeared as a big piece of rock jutting out of the Aegean Sea, not the verdant paradise that I had imagined. The taxi to Agios Kirykos navigated one sharp turn after another with practiced maneuvers. There seemed no straight stretches on that two-lane road and I got only fleeting glimpses of scenery: a mountain on one side and on the other, a scrubby, dusty landscape leading down to the sea. Near occasional houses in the distance stood rows of beehives, too many to count. I was eager to walk the lanes, to see close up what was growing, but first my husband and I needed to get settled in our apartment in Agios Kirykos, the capital. A small working town with a harbor for ferries and little boats, most local businesses, shops and a handful of restaurants are located there.

Our first meal at one of the nameless outdoor restaurants by the harbor provided a glimpse of many meals to come. We were given a menu, but not all of the items were always available. Traditional Ikarian dishes such as tomatoes and peppers stuffed with rice, the farmers salad and soufico—any combination of vegetables, particularly eggplant, peppers, onions, garlic and zucchini–could generally be ordered. One evening we were treated to gigantes, giant beans cooked with tomatoes and herbs. At the nearby village of Therma I ordered fried okra and tiny fried fish. On the north side of the island, in Evdilos, I enjoyed an unusual preparation of sardines which were split open and fried. I also asked for the wild greens pie listed on the menu. The apologetic young server said she would ask her mother if it was available. Quickly, I responded that I did not want to impose. Graciously, Mom acquiesced to my request and agreed to defrost and bake a slice for me. So worth the wait, the deliciousness of that traditional dish: the flaky phyllo like crust encased a combina-tion of wild greens. The varieties I could not identify (possibly purslane, arugula, dandelion) but unmis-takable were the hints of mint and oregano.

Back in town, the restaurant below our apartment, under a grapevine canopy, appeared to be a family affair also. My husband and I enjoyed guessing the makeup of this family as no one spoke English. We thought grandfather to be the older gentleman who silently showed us our sausages before he cooked them on the outdoor grill behind our table. Was the respectful teenager, who was our waiter, his grandson? I saw "grandmother" emerge briefly from the house to indicate that the stuffed peppers and fried *saganaki* cheese were ready. My husband described their house wine, a rosé, colored pale orange and served in a carafe, as dry with good depth. I simply thought it was good.

It was easy to focus on food when I first arrived. Though many of the dishes were new to me, I was a little surprised at how much I liked everything that I had eaten. However, I knew that a long and satisfying life had to include more. Besides their diet, there was much more to learn about the Ikarians. Because the island is primarily mountainous, historically isolated and vulnerable to predatory pirates, most of the population once lived only in those mountains. They learned to do with little. Out of necessity they were self-sufficient and developed close relationships within their communities. These conditions still prevail. Even today Ikarians seem to use everything that will grow or live on their island. Individual gardens are the sources for fruits and vegetable that they harvest when fully ripe. They forage for greens to cook and plants to dry for tea. Meat comes from grazing, grass-fed animals (sheep, goats, pigs), and they make their own breads and cheeses.

The island is renowned for the quality and variety of its honey. The rare Anama honey is from bees that feast on mountain heather: Once it leaves the island it is advertised as a superfood. The Mountain Tea—from the Sideritis plant—is said to be a defense against Alzheimer's Disease. Locals think the daily cups of herbal tea contribute to longevity. Many of these claims have been backed up by extensive research. Moreover, the Ikarian lifestyle includes, out of necessity, plenty of exercise, and as I understand it, a daily nap.

I made a point to walk the neighborhoods in town, seeing many gardens squeezed into the smallest spaces. In one plot, only five-by-fifteen feet adjacent to a house, several lemon trees grew, a tiny vegetable garden thrived and grapevines covered the fence. Along the road, I loved the scent of bushes of wild thyme in full purple bloom and covered with bees. Most mornings I finished my walk at the Alecafe. While writing and enjoying my coffee under the trees outside, I watched groups of men sitting for hours at tables near me talking, prompting me to wonder what could they be talking about for so long and enthusiastically? Later in the afternoon, I could hear the tap-tapping sounds of several backgammon games. Evenings, women and children filled the square.

Mothers sat together and chatted while their children never ceased finding friends and things to do. All day long I observed people who seemed relaxed and happy as they interacted with each other.

One afternoon, in a cafe high above the sea enjoying the view, I had a conversation with the woman owner. I had heard that many people who were born on Ikaria and had moved away, returned. She was one of them, and as I sipped my ouzo, she told me the following story: A man from Ikaria who was badly injured in the Second World War, went to the United States for treatment, which was successful. He stayed there, married and raised a family. But in his early sixties, he got a diagnosis of cancer, confirmed by several doctors. He decided to return to Ikaria to die. His decision was primarily based on the fact that burial services would not cost his family as much there as it would in America. He and his wife settled in easily. Eventually feeling well enough, he planted his own garden and joined others in community gatherings. He was over a hundred years old when he died.

On Ikaria a significant number of people live to be ninety and older. Is it because of their all-embracing lifestyle, their diet, their sense of belonging along with a sense of purpose or something else? The taxi driver, who drove me from Agios Kyigos to Evdilos, seemed to take such pleasure in his job. Admittedly he loved driving his Mercedes like a race car, always with the windows down because, he said, he loved the scent of seasonal flowers. I, too, noted that the shrubs of Spartium (broom), crowding the side of the road, were a mass of vibrant yellow that day with an intense aroma to match.

I began asking many people their own ideas about what contributes to a long life. When I asked that question of the bartender at the café, she suggested it's because of how people help each other. While in the herb shop, looking for teas and honey, I asked the shopkeeper what she thought the secret is, and she replied, "It's to be calm." A young man who likes to cook thinks the secret is in the water: water for drinking, as well as the water in vegetables. Dan Buettner says that people simply forget to die. I don't think there's one definitive or easy answer. No one mentioned genetics.

A bronze sculpture of Icarus stands in the small island airport. He is poised to "take off". I think of my grandson poised, ready to begin the next stage of his life as he begins college. He'll be interested in my Ikarian adventure, intrigued by my "blue zone" experience. He'll ask me questions. I'll answer honestly that I cannot create a life exactly as I found it on Ikaria, which is a unique and self-contained environment. I live in a congested suburban neighborhood, not on an island of 8,500 people. But there are ideas–even habits–I can incorporate into my life in Maryland. My sources for food are the local organic market that is within walking distance. I have a small vegetable and herb garden and I can recreate soufico using my own oregano, mint and basil. I intend to perfect the recipe for zucchini fritters that is now one of my favorite dishes. I'll make them when the family gathers this weekend. I brought home a supply of mountain heather honey, enough to share. I know I will be more mindful and grateful for the joy that comes from our family being together and how much it contributes to all our lives. I am also thinking about young Icarus and all my grandchildren and how I admire their enthusiasm and optimism. An old woman, wings still intact, can still learn from them all.

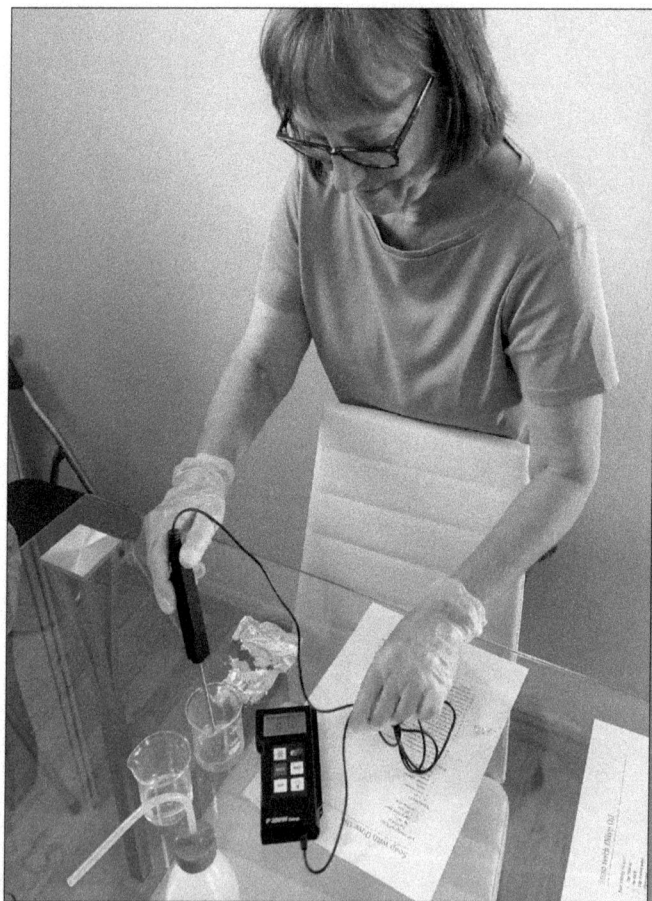

The author conducting her extra virgin experiment

My Extra Virgin Experiment

Laurie McAndish King

I have a thing for extra virgin olive oil. Some might call it an obsession, but I prefer to think of it as a love affair. I've chased that golden-green elixir around the world, savoring its subtle inflections: grassy, fruity, nutty. My husband has waited patiently in elegant tasting rooms as I sipped varietals and cultivars and single-estate standouts, robust early harvests and pale, buttery award-winners.

At home, extra virgin olive oil is my favorite afternoon snack. I pour it onto a cracker and admire it there in a tiny, shimmering pool surrounded by a dollop of hummus to keep it from falling off. After all, it is the olive oil I'm after. Its leafy hue reminds me of hot summer afternoons. Its peppery burn lashes mischievously at the back of my tongue. Its light viscosity slides luxuriously down my throat. It moistens my lips and glistens on my chin. I smooth the excess onto my hands and elbows. I'm often tempted to smother every inch of my body with the unctuous condiment. I did that once and felt like an awesome Greek goddess ... until the fruit flies started circling. It also made my sheets smell somewhat rancid—a decidedly ungoddess-like effect.

It's not surprising then, with this obsession, that from the minute I started planning my Greek vacation I knew the exotic liquid would have to play a part in the experience. Olive oil is a crucial part of the Mediterranean diet, which is said to support a long and healthy life. It may be the fresh fruits and vegetables, whole grains, legumes, fish and moderate amounts of red wine that actually produce the desired effect, but I prefer to think it's all about the olive oil. Anti-inflammatory, high in phytonutrients and anti-oxidants, and helpful in preventing maladies as varied as Alzheimer's disease, breast cancer, high blood pressure, obesity, stroke, and type 2 diabetes, it could probably replace one's primary care physician. It has even been credited with enlarging breasts when applied properly.

In fact, olive oil has played an important part in the human experience for millennia. Kırkpınar, or olive oil wrestling, is the world's oldest documented sporting event, dating back at least to 2600 BCE, and is recognized by UNESCO as an Intangible Cultural Heritage. But, in my opinion, olive oil has played its most significant role in human experience as an ingredient in soap. Without soap, we'd still be licking our own skin to get rid of the dust and dirt of everyday life, which might be good for lingual dexterity, but would have set us far, far behind in terms of making time for innovations and inventions, not to mention government, art and critical thinking. One could even make the argument that soap is the foundation upon which civilization has been built.

According to one legend, soap originated on the island of Lesbos, where animal sacrifice was practiced. The remains of those sacrifices—fat and ashes—flowed from stone altars into the river when rains were heavy. Women washing their clothes in the river noticed how good the laundry looked after their oblations, made the connection between animal fat and cleanliness, and soap was invented. The poet Sappho, one of the first to chronicle the efficacy of soap, is supposedly the namesake of soap making or *saponification*. It being Greece, folks quickly figured out that olive oil was a more convenient ingredient than sacrificial animal fat, and so began the long history of olive oil soap making. And one of the best places to make olive oil soap, I discovered, is on a Greek island.

After a week in Athens—seven days spent slathering my innards in delicious olive oil—I flew to Crete. From the capital city of Heraklion I hopped a local bus to Knossos, the famed site of spectacular ancient ruins, where I encountered evidence of olive oil's importance in ancient times. There, a prominent grouping of gigantic terracotta amphorae—once containing hundreds of gallons olive oil—huddle together like friends frozen in timeless conversation. Nearby, I came across a fresco of elegant Mycenaean maidens dancing in front of olive trees. As I admired the image, my wizened guide, Charidinos, extolled the virtues of olive oil with irrefutable logic: "*Elia* means *olive tree*, or *tree of wisdom*, in Greek," he explained. "So you see, two or three spoons of olive oil every day will make the mind sharp and the body strong!"

Back in Heraklion I discovered yet another way to enjoy the oil of my dreams. I decided to take a class in olive oil soap making. It would be the perfect finale to my Greek explorations. I was pretty sure I remembered that soap making requires lye, or some other highly caustic chemical, but the instructor, Gregory, was a chemist when he wasn't teaching tourists to make soap, so I figured he'd be well-versed in safety. Besides, I could give the soap as a gift to my son's girlfriend, Debbie, who loves fragrant lotions and skin care products. I hadn't found a gift for her yet, and this would be truly Grecian. It would also be an expression of my affection, since it would demonstrate that I'd taken time—several hours, in fact—from my peregrinations to do something thoughtful for her. I signed up.

I expected the soap-making experience to take place either in a chemistry lab or in a small cottage with an ancient stone altar surrounded by trees and friendly woodland animals. But the taxi delivered me to an apartment in the suburbs. Two young couples joined me for the class; one couple was from Scotland, the other from Germany. Apparently there's a worldwide interest among young people in soap production ... or in extra virgin olive oil ... or maybe in making thoughtful little gifts to bring home from Greek vacations.

Besides being a chemist, Gregory—in his thirties, a little overweight, with a headful of beautiful black hair—played in a band. Ikea-like furniture and several guitars crowded his living room. He had set up a small worktable in the kitchen, which had acid green walls. They were the color olives would be if they were electrified, and created a vague feeling of danger. The supplies Gregory had laid out added to the ambiance of peril: Each participant was provided with a pair of protective goggles, rubber gloves, a 4-inch square of aluminum foil to measure ingredients onto, a beaker, and a long glass stirring rod. We all shared a scale and digital thermometer.

It looked quite scientific. In fact, it reminded me of chemistry class—not a good memory. Despite being excellent at following directions, I could never get my experiments to come out the proper way. That is to say, even though they were "experiments," there were still expectations. Often my results were not even close to the normal range—so much so that I began to wonder whether a fellow classmate was sneaking into the lab and sabotaging my careful work, perhaps trying to influence the grading curve to his or her advantage. That's the way I prefer to explain my consistently un-satisfactory results. And that's why I never really liked chemistry. I *wanted* to like it. I loved the idea of mixing exotic ingredients, like an alchemist turning lead into gold, or a witch brewing up love potions—but I was clearly not cut out for it.

So when Gregory gave us a quick chemistry lesson, it went completely over my head. It began with something about micellar aggregates of surfactant molecules dispersed in colloid liquids and the packing behavior of single-tail lipids in a bilayer, sequestering the hydrophobic regions ... and it ended with the fact that soap made from pure olive oil is known to be especially mild.

Gregory also gave us a safety lesson. "It's important to measure all the quantities carefully," he explained, "and to follow my directions exactly. If the ingredients are combined in the wrong order or in incorrect amounts or even at the wrong temperatures, you could end up with both heat burns and chemical burns. Or with an explosion that would decimate my kitchen!"

Gregory held up a small square of aluminum foil from a previous soap-making class. It was burned—perhaps *dissolved* would be a better term, for only half of it remained—where a caustic chemical sitting on the foil square had come into contact with water. We all gasped appropriately.

I donned the safety goggles and volunteered to go first. With Gregory supervising, I combined the initial ingredients and stirred them carefully with the glass rod. The solution clouded and bubbled, then cleared as a chemical reaction heated the beaker until it was so hot it nearly melted my latex gloves. While the class waited for it to cool off, Gregory gave us a concise history lesson: The earliest recorded evidence of the production of soap-like substances dates back to around 2800 BCE in ancient Babylon. Liquid soap was not invented, however, until late in the nineteenth century. In 1898, a man named B.J. Johnson developed a mixture derived from palm and olive oils, and introduced Palmolive brand soap.

While Gregory talked, my solution was cooling off and ready for the next step. "Do you want to add color or scent?" he asked, pulling out small bottles of red and blue coloring. I considered the options. This was an important decision. I wanted it to be just right, but wasn't sure what Debbie would like best. *Hmmm,* I thought, *something pretty and feminine, for sure.*

Finally, I chose red, figuring I'd add just one drop to turn the mixture a delicate, rosy hue. I'd create a pretty pink bar that was exceptionally soothing and moisturizing. Several scents were available, too: yummy chocolate or healing lavender. I decided on the chocolate. I'd had a chocolate massage once in Spain, and it was an absolutely luscious experience. Excited about my decision, I could already envision Debbie lathering up with wonderful pink, chocolate-scented bubbles.

I added the color carefully, following Gregory's instructions. But I didn't get pink. It turns out that adding just one teeny, tiny drop of red to an extra-green, extra-virgin olive oil solution immediately turns it an unappealing shade of brown. And adding the chocolate scent made it clump together—suddenly the whole thing went "off" like a curdled brown hollandaise. I attempted to transfer my "soap" into the mold, but the lumpy mess continued to congeal and wouldn't pour. I had to scoop it out with my awkwardly gloved hands and dump it into the rectangular mold, poking it like lumpy mashed potatoes into the corners. That old chemistry-class curse had followed me all the way to Crete! I persevered, doing my best to flatten the top, to make it look like a beautiful little gem that Debbie would be proud to put on her bathroom sink. But in the end, there was no escaping the fact that it was brown and lumpy, and looked very much like a ... well, like a thing that belongs in another place in the bathroom, a thing that should be flushed ... and never seen again.

What will they think when I try to bring it home through Customs? I worried. I would definitely have some explaining to do. Perhaps Gregory could provide me a certificate of authenticity. And what would Debbie think? I couldn't possibly give her a gift that looked like *you know what.*

After seeing my unfortunate creation, the German and Scottish couples decided to keep their soaps pure and free of any added color or scent. Of course, their bars turned out beautifully: silky smooth in texture, pale Palmolive-green colored, and with a naturally fresh, clean scent.

I left feeling discouraged—clearly an incompetent chemist, a total failure at what should have been a simple process. I had nothing for Debbie. And my homeward flight was first thing in the morning.

As I walked back to my hotel I kept an eye out for souvenirs in Heraklion's countless gift shops, which sold tie-dyed clothing, olive-themed ceramics, and soaps—lots of olive oil soaps in bright, clear colors: lavender, peach, strawberry red, sea-mist green. The scents were lovely, too: vanilla, lemon, jasmine. I chose a pretty yellow, honey-scented bar for Debbie. I hope she likes it.

I gave the brown one to my husband.

Thanasis Maskaleris on the Island of Crete

AEOLUS

Linda Watanabe McFerrin

for Thanasis

The wind had come up.
It howled round the island.
"Aeolus loosing his wine skin," you said.
It screamed under the doors
raising dust, small puffs on the floor,
pushed across stones.

Asses brayed shakily.
Every windowpane rattled.
No light, only candles,
white in the darkness, the socks on our feet,
as we lined up to say our sleepy farewells.

That night, when you left us, no planes flew.
The winds had shut down the island.
No vessels sailed out
(the Furies were cheated)
into the back night under full sail,
into the hungry mouth of the sea.

137

Minotaur sculpture by Stuart Wolfe

DREAMING THE MINOTAUR

Laurie McAndish King

Knossos lies in ruin, yet it is stunning. Blocks of glinting white stone have crumbled to the ground, leaving a sprawling, sugar-cube outline where the palace's walls once towered. Bright red reconstructions replace the original stout cypress columns on endless colonnades; faded frescoes evoke the citadel's elegant past. Once the capital of a flourishing Minoan civilization, this ancient site is now a tourist attraction. I had come to Knossos, on the island of Crete, in search of a labyrinth. Actually, I wanted to find *the* labyrinth—Knossos was said to be home to the world's very first.

I secretly hoped that walking the labyrinth would help me with a life-long problem: difficulty making decisions. My father taught me from the time I was very young to think for myself. But, like many men, he became irritated when my opinion differed from his. "There are only two answers," he would say. "Mine, and the wrong one." He pretended it was a joke, but it wasn't. Then there was Mom, a genius at looking at every issue from multiple angles. Together they were perfect-storm parents for raising me, a daughter who is skilled at considering endless perspectives, easily intuits what others think ... and second-guesses her own opinions so thoroughly she's often unsure whether she even *has* a personal point of view. Growing up this way got me thinking about the mysteries of how we know, and how we decide. What are the relative weights of analysis and instinct, the merits of reason and emotion? I hoped that figuring out the interplay between confidence and faith—those two opposing cornerstones of conclusion—would transform my wobbly decision-making abilities. That is what drew me to Knossos.

I would make a pilgrimage to the original labyrinth and have a magical experience there—attending only to earth and sky, feeling the subtleties of air and light as they played off one another, silencing my monkey-mind chatter. I would walk the labyrinth until I felt what I needed: *confidence* to take the next step, even if I didn't know exactly where I was going, and *faith* that I could enter the unknown and find a way back out. My indecision would be transformed into certainty!

That was my plan.

Knossos, just a short bus ride from Crete's capital city of Heraklion, is a lovely place to wander. The palace once looked out over rolling hills blanketed with olive groves. Their gnarled descendants still cloak the landscape and are home to finches and flycatchers, to warblers and robins and wrens. Beneath the trees' silvery leaves, golden grasses shimmer in the heat, cicadas thrum, and Queen Anne's lace folds its delicate blossoms into thick vegetal cups.

I arrived in the morning, intending to be in and out before the summer heat became too debilitating. The place was immense. Stone walls outlined the remains of private apartments, interior and exterior courtyards, complex baths, granaries, storage rooms and meeting halls—all linked by wide walkways and the palace's four flights of staircases. Waves of light shimmered, mirage-like, as the sun rose higher in the sky, its bright glare reflecting on acres of white stone. Map in hand, I explored the architecture as it repeated and reflected, twisting in upon itself and confusing even the most observant visitor. But where was the actual labyrinth? I wandered for several hours, looking high and low, gamely following winding pathways, hopefully poking my head over and over again into the same rooms, which looked different from their various approaches.

Finally I realized the truth.

There *was* no labyrinth at Knossos. In all likelihood, there never had been. The labyrinth I'd turned to for salvation was a myth, just like the Minotaur who supposedly lived inside it. My aspirations puddled in the heat.

Maybe it was the too-bright sunlight, alternating with deep shadows in the porticoed throne room. Perhaps it was the larger-than-life-sized frescoed griffons inside, their graceful lion-bodies and bird-heads detailed with mesmerizing spirals. Or the blue monkey with a long nose, stooping by the side of a river to pluck a tall stalk of papyrus. The frescoes' dreamlike imagery pulled at my imagination as I wandered the ruins. Most of the images were of lotus blossoms and long-limbed courtiers, but one was unique. It depicts an oddly red and freakishly acrobatic youth somersaulting over the back of a huge brown bull—*bull-jumping*, in the parlance of the time. Two older boys stand nearby, their black hair in long ringlets, their powerful thighs only partly covered by loincloths. One of the boys stands with his arms outstretched, ready to catch the vaulting athlete; the other stands directly in front of the charging beast, his chest right in between its long, curving horns. The bull's straining neck and forequarters are exaggerated, suggesting their immense strength. The bull itself arches as he powers forward, clearly excited by the affair. Light-headed in the heat,

141

gazing at the bull-jumper framed by dizzying geometrics, I entered the Minotaur's world and began to hear his thoughts…

I smelled it even before the darkness shifted—a softening of the sour air, dampening the dusty floor ever so slightly, relaxing my nostrils, calming the fury that is my constant companion. Rain was coming. Queen Pasiphae was on her way, too. She occasionally visited me in secret, winding through the labyrinth in the dead of night, or sometimes during a storm. Always in the dark. Even she, who had borne and nurtured me, taught me to walk, raised me from infant calf to bull—even my mother was afraid of me now. I could smell her fear, arcing like lightning in the air.

The problem was my lust for blood. Seven maidens, seven boys. Every year, ever since my adolescent hormones began their violent surge. At first I didn't care whether they were virgins, but that's what King Minos always sent, and that's what I came to expect. I can only imagine how the king felt about me, his grotesque son, with the body of a boy and the head and tail of a bull. My very name was a combination of his own—Minos—and Taurus, a reference to the bovine who was my biological father. I was a constant reminder of the queen's infidelity, of her maddening obsession with the majestic white bull. It infuriated the king. For a while he turned to other women, but the queen was a powerful sorceress, and cast a spell on Minos so he was doomed to ejaculate centipedes, scorpions and serpents whenever he lay with a concubine. Not surprisingly, they proved fatal to his favorite mistresses.

To be fair, the queen—I was never allowed to call her "Mother," never allowed to have a mother, really—was not solely at fault. The king had owed a debt to the gods, and his queen was made to pay the price. A victim of divinely inflicted desire, she fell hopelessly in love with the handsome white bull, was overcome with passion, and became pregnant with what turned out to be me. The entire affair doubtless made the king feel brutish. Pasiphae nourished me at her breast when I was young, which must have been embarrassment enough, but when I hit adolescence and developed a taste for human flesh, the king could no longer disguise his contempt; he banished me to the labyrinth.

It was a vast subterranean prison—so dark I went blind in its depths, so endlessly circuitous it induced constant nausea and despair, so utterly terrifying it was surely the gateway to hell. And it was my home.

"Mother?" I dared to call out for her. To call her "Mother." I felt so lonely.

Silence.

"Mother, where are you?"

I felt her breath nearby. Light, like a breeze. Cool, compared to my own dank exhalations. Would she speak to me?

"Mother, how long must I live in this tortuous chamber?"

Finally Pasiphae spoke. "There is no answer," she said. "Seek it lovingly."

This epigram roused me from my reverie as the day's heat filled my lungs. It had not been hard to morph into the Minotaur. I'd had my share of black spells, of swift descent, of wandering blindly, unable to claw my way out of confusion and despair. I knew how the Minotaur felt: dead end after dead end, nowhere to turn, helpless to do anything but wait. Hoping the darkness would lift, by some unknown grace, and light would return.

With that thought I realized, startled, that I had discovered the labyrinth after all. It was not a hilltop cakewalk, well-trodden by seekers and tourists, nor a sacred space in the halls of a great cathedral. It was not the palace complex at Knossos, but rather my confusing psychological journey through it—the journey that led, finally, to my daydream of the Minotaur and his mother's wise counsel.

> *There is no answer. Seek it lovingly.*
> —Socrates

My own mother had framed these very words, penned in her easy, rhythmic handwriting, and posted them as a prayer on the bookshelf above her desk. *Let go of the need for certainty. The opposite is not indecision; it's openness, curiosity, willingness to accept complexity.* My mother knew this. And just as Minotaur's mother had saved him—or at least comforted him—in the face of his father's rejection, my own mother had posted these words as a comfort. They had emerged from my subconscious in the voice of another mother whose child was lost and lonely—and as a reminder of the infinite entanglement that is the labyrinth, and the wisdom of adopting its lesson of embracing paradox.

Cist grave at Pavlopetri underwater archaeological site

ETERNAL PAVLOPETRI

Barbara J. Euser

The sailors breathed a sigh of relief as they rounded Cape Malea, and the wind shifted to the south. It would be clear sailing now to the port town of Pavlopetri. The hills of Elafonisos were clearly visible on their left. The mountainous northern boundary of the Bay rose on their right. All they had to do was steer straight to the end of the long, narrow bay to the sandy beaching area at its western end. Cape Malea was notorious for its storms and conflicting currents. At the point where the Ionian Sea meets the Aegean Sea, sailors often encountered challenging conditions. But today the weather had cooperated, and they would soon reach their home port.

It had been a successful voyage. They had traded the textiles woven in Pavlopetri for some lovely pottery. They had acquired a new venerable icon for the temple: a small beautifully crafted figurine of a goddess. Their voyage had taken them to Crete, where they had observed the powerful—and intrusive—Minoan government of Knossos in action, another reason to be happy to be heading home to their independent city.

Each sailor dreamed of that evening's celebration. For some, it would be coming home to his own family: a chance to be surrounded by his wife and children. Others were returning to their parents' homes. For the captain and the navigator, the celebration would be an official welcome from the mayor of Pavlopetri, also leader of the surrounding agricultural region.

In 3,000 BCE, when the sailors reached their homes at Pavlopetri, the town covered about eight hectares of land. It comprised one-and two-story buildings of adobe walls built on stone foundations. Streets of houses were built around courtyards, and a large administrative center dominated the town. Warehouses stockpiled terra cotta pithoi filled with olives, olive oil, grain, wine and honey.

As I walk along the beach today, I dream of those ancient mariners. On the hills overlooking the Bay, sheep and goats graze on grasses and short shrubs, just as they did 5,000 years ago. Olive trees and grapevines, cotton, wheat, onions and other vegetables all grow well in the soil near Pavlopetri. Buyers from Spain and Italy purchase local olive oil to add flavor to their milder oil. Farmers still grow onions and other vegetables. They tend honeybees, gather honey and ferment mead. They harvest their grapes and ferment wine. The olives and olive oil, garden vegetables, honey and wine that I consume today, all link me with the people who lived in Pavlopetri.

These days, Pavlopetri is submerged in two to three meters of water. It sank gradually, at the rate of about one meter every thousand years, and by 1,600 BCE, Pavlopetri had disappeared. Two thousand years is a long time for a port to survive and develop. From a navigational standpoint, it had an extremely favorable location. It was undoubtedly a very important port town. The foundations of the streets, courtyards and buildings, as well as the thousands of findings archeologists have uncovered, reveal the story. Hundreds of loom weights tell of a thriving textile production; pottery shards from Thessaloniki, Crete, Sicily and Cyprus indicate trade routes; a bronze goddess figurine speaks of religion.

From the time Pavlopetri disappeared in 1,600 BCE until recent times, the significance of the submerged ruins was unrecognized. Local people knew that something had been located there, and nearly everyone had pottery fragments from the site in their homes.

In 1968, Dr. Nicholas Flemming was travelling through the Peloponnese, looking for ancient port sites. He had nothing but his understanding of sailing and navigation to guide him. When he saw Vatika Bay, he thought *what a marvelous protected area at its western end.* He took his snorkeling gear and checked it out. What he found, amazed him. He stayed at the site for weeks. He used a measuring stick to create a basic map of the ruins. His observation and logic had led him to an archeological site of large dimensions.

In 1969, a team from Cambridge University, led by Dr. Anthony Harding, came to Pavlopetri to map the site. They discovered even more foundations, and added to Flemming's map.

Separately, Dr. Aggelos Delavorias of the Greek Ministry of Culture's Department of Lakonian Antiquities came to Neapolis on a gathering mission. He went from house to house asking the local inhabitants if they had any pieces of pottery or other items they had gathered from the western end of Vatika Bay, now recognized as the archeological site of Pavlopetri. He gathered wheelbarrows full of pottery. The Municipality of Neapolis offered to store the huge number of items until the Ministry of Culture could receive them. Over generations, the site had been very effectively cleaned—looted of surface artifacts. Dr. Delacovias' collection of findings from Pavlopetri is now stored at the Ministry of Culture in Athens.

After the initial excitement of Flemming's discovery, nothing happened at Pavlopetri for the next forty years. In 2009, the Ministry of Culture awarded a five-year permit for the excavation and mapping of Pavlopetri to the University of Nottingham. The team, led by Dr. Jon Henderson and Dr. Cynthia Gallou, in cooperation with Dr. Elias Spondilis of the Ministry of Culture's Department of Underwater Antiquities, brought an international group of scientists to Pavlopetri. The University of Sydney's contingent, led by Dr. Oscar Pizarro, was responsible for mapping Pavlopetri, using the most up-to-date techniques. Their unmanned robotic vehicle mapped Pavlopetri in stereoscope and transmitted the images directly to the computers of the scientists headquartered at the local Greek taverna nearby. Dr. Nicholas Flemming joined the group.

Simultaneously, the Hellenic Center for Marine Research, under the direction of Dr. Dimitris Sakellariou, carried out a study of the sea floor of Vatika Bay. The geologists from HCMR were looking at the potential reason for the submersion of the ancient port. The question was: Did the sea level rise, or did the sea floor sink? The geologists' answer is that the sea floor gradually sank, as the tectonic plates located to the east of Vatika Bay slowly, slowly shifted in relation to each other.

That shift in tectonic plates also turned Elafonisos into an island. In 1968, when Flemming arrived on the scene, Elafonisos was an island, although 5,500 years ago, it was connected to the mainland. The stone outcroppings that barely rise above the surface of the Bay just north of the islet of Pavlopetri were part of a ridge that protected the city from the north winds. The two large chamber tombs, which one can now swim into, were dug into the ridge. Boats would have entered the port of Pavlopetri from the south, beaching on the smooth sands of Pounta Beach.

The University of Sydney published the results of its sophisticated mapping work immediately. A whole new section of the town had been revealed. The University of Nottingham has yet to publish its findings from its excavations. According to its permit, it has ten years from the end of the permit in which to do so, which will be 2024.

Scientists identified the largest threats to the preservation and protection of Pavlopetri as shifting sediments, anchoring and fishing by small boats at the site, pollution, and looting. To assist the Ministry of Culture in coping with these problems, the U.S. non-profit organization the Alliance for the Restoration of Cultural Heritage, through its Greek chapter, raised the money to purchase eleven buoys, which were donated to the Ministry of Culture. In 2016, during the first Pavlopetri Watch Day, an event supported by the World Monuments Fund to raise awareness about Pavlopetri, Dr. Aggeliki Simosi, Director of the Department of Underwater Antiquities, placed the buoys around the perimeter of the site. Dr. Nicholas Flemming attended the ceremony, which was conducted on a traditional wooden boat, a caique. The concept was to alert small boats to the existence of the archeological site and warn them to keep out of it. In less than one year, all the buoys had disappeared. Greek ARCH replaced them with much cheaper buoys, which also quickly disappeared. The Ministry of Culture gave up on that idea.

The threat of pollution to the existing ruins comes from two sources: the large commercial ships that anchor in Vatika Bay, and runoff of fungicides and pesticides used by local farmers. There is no Special Port Regulation (SPR) governing Vatika Bay. A proposed SPR allowing an unlimited number of ships to anchor in the Bay encountered the outrage of all the hotel owners, restaurants, bars, and cafes that make their living from the sustainable coastal tourism economy. That plan was shelved. Another plan, proposed by a former head of the Coast Guard in Neapolis would limit the number of ships anchored in a very specific part of the Bay to two ships a day during nine months of the year and no ships during June, July, and August; limit the activities the ships could carry out while in the Bay; and limit the length of stay to two days. That SPR, although enjoying the support of the majority of the local population, has yet to be approved.

In 2017, the Ministry of Culture delineated the boundaries of the Pavlopetri archeological site and in February 2018, they were published in the official Greek government gazette, called the F.E.K. Based on that publication, the Greek Coast Guard and the Hydrological Service collaborated in having the boundaries of the Pavlopetri archeological site included on all official marine charts. This was the first time a Greek underwater archeological site had appeared on a marine chart.

In 2019, during Pavlopetri Watch Day, the Ministry of Culture presented its proposed Management Plan for Pavlopetri. It includes signage, a designated parking area, wooden walkways to protect the fragile sand dune ecosystem, and an informational kiosk. Interagency consultations regarding the Management Plan are scheduled for fall 2019.

The Greek Coast Guard, which has a station in Neapolis, has been given authority to monitor the coastal area included in the boundaries of the Pavlopetri archeological site. Camping is illegal in Greek archeological sites. The Coast Guard has succeeded in shooing away many of the trailers overnighting in the site.

As of 2019, there are four signs on the highway pointing the way to Pavlopetri. There are no signs at the site itself.

At each of the four Pavlopetri Watch Days 2016-2019, guided snorkeling tours led by the Ministry of Culture have attracted dozens of participants. There is great interest in the site from tourists and locals alike. But there is no way for tourists to identify or understand what the rows of carefully placed submerged stones mean.

What does the future hold for Pavlopetri? The Ministry of Culture has made it clear that it does not intend to authorize further excavation of the site. This is consistent with the philosophy that excavation inevitably destroys a site at the same time it discovers more about it. Some sites must be left for future generations of archeologists to explore. The existing ruins are easily accessible, but require explanation and interpretation in order to be appreciated by tourists. The Ministry of Culture has proposed creating a self-guided tour with laminated maps and a few signed locations. This could also be accomplished via virtual tours that visitors could view online before they begin snorkeling. Before any development starts, there is an opportunity to create a nearly unspoiled site by limiting vehicle access all along the beach from Pounta to Mangano—the full length of the coastline of the designated archeological site. With appropriate care, Pavlopetri could become an important tourist attraction, bolstering the coastal tourism economy, and sparking the imagination of every child and adult who snorkels over the foundations of streets, courtyards and homes.

I would like to know more about the people who lived in Pavlopetri. As I snorkel over the ruins of their homes, I feel the relief of a sailor when he beaches his boat, walks up the street and crosses the lintel into his house. I feel the loss of the parents who buried their baby in a cist grave in a wall. I feel the bustle of the marketplace, the rhythm of working at a loom, the tedium of a warehouse clerk keeping track of pithoi full of olives and grain. There is much we do not know about the lives of the people who lived in Pavlopetri, and much is left to discover. However, one thing I do know: Our lives are interconnected, fundamentally the same, and when I swim above Pavlopetri, when I ponder its success, demise, and preservation, the centuries disappear, and I am simply there in a very special place that links me to other people, other times.

Mosaic at St. Nectarios Greek Orthodox Church
on the island of Aegina

WHAT MY FATHER DREAMS

Joanna Biggar

"The sleep of the dead is so deep that all who walk it dream…"
—Henry Miller, *The Colossus of Maroussi*

I have come here, Father,
your new ashes still unscattered,
to seek the way of the living.
Yet in every sleep I find your face,
your dream.

You traveled once to this honeyed land
and brought me a golden necklace,
finely woven as Athena's hair.
I came after, and brought you
as my gift

a holy icon in three parts,
saintly faces edged with gold.
Unfolded, it sat on your desk

shining with that light from
another world.

Now I have returned
and the light of all Greece shines
on your face—your photo, my icon—
as if ready to speak.
But what are you dreaming now?

That although this land is not
our land, still I might find you
here, in this place where
the living and the dead are
not afraid to meet?

That although these seas are not
our seas, when I swim in waters
clear as the color of God's blue eye,
I feel you here, too,
swimming along with me?

Or that under every living rock
Upended, there is a story you forgot to tell
whispered through the oleanders and palms,
like the ones on the street in California
where you were born?

Or perhaps when I sail,
not as a warrior like you,
but as a seeker, crossing

the secrets of the sunken city
lost on that Lakonian Sea,

I will find among its shimmering towers
and golden fishes, its treasures,
gone but to the realm of imagining,
your spirit,
alive and speaking

from that watery tomb.
There, where past and present flow together,
and gods and angels spin
the silken threads of
mortals' lives

There, Father, I will walk deep with you,
hear your voice,
your dreams,
and sleep again
the bearable sleep of the living.

The author's photo of an octopus on a vase
at the Acropolis Museum

KNOW THYSELF: THE OCTOPUS AND ME

MJ Pramik

I used to eat octopus. In fact, I used to *love* eating octopus—grilled or ceviche—until I learned these soft-bodied mollusks get amorous on ecstasy. Yes, ecstasy: the drug. Scientists at Johns Hopkins University recently dosed a consortium (collective name for a group of octopus) of the eight-armed creatures with the drug we call methylenedioxymethamphetamine, MDMA, Molly, X, or candy. Researchers discovered that when given a high dose of the drug, the treated invertebrates would huddle alone in a corner of their tank. But when dosed with a small quantity—the equivalent amount to what a human would ingest—that same octopus transformed into an empathetic, cuddly social being.

When placed in an aquarium together, octopuses usually demonstrate aggressive behavior to tank mates. They color shift, turn dark hues, cobalt blue or ink black. The attacker stands tall on several tentacles, often shooting a solitary appendage towards its adversary, lashing out much like the way they're depicted in horror films. But ecstasy-treated octopuses sidle up to their fellow cephalopods, slowly exploring the environment, caressing toys, using several arms. These responses strikingly resemble human behavioral changes when on the drug. In people, ecstasy decreases anxiety and inhibitions, generates empathy and compassion, and enriches the physical senses. In octopuses, the investigators witnessed a monster of the deep, long-considered aggressive, become an affectionate creature, full of touchy-feely strokes for rivals.

After reading the study, I couldn't help but seek out documentary evidence of these incredible findings. My inner scientist simply had to know what octopus "love behaviors" looked like.

Little did I know that my quick online video search would deter me from ever again eating an octopus. A plethora of films abound of octopus caresses. But I found so much more: an octopus unscrewing a jar, mimicking a flounder, and, most precious of all, pretending to be a piece of coral.

One video showed a rather large golden brown octopus sliding in the surf along with a family who had rescued this creature the day before. The animal had come back to the same beach and spent an hour with them as they strolled across the sand. Another recording revealed a small octopus being released into the ocean after having been stranded at low tide, then returning to thank the human who released it. The octopod placed its tentacle gently atop the foot of its savior, stayed still for a minute as if in silent prayer, then pushed out to the sea. Heart-rending.

This simple act of connection and cross-species empathy nailed shut the coffin of my octopus-eating days. My throat tightened, stomach clenched, no more. I could never be at ease with eating octopus again.

My culinary sea change has evolved, as in any evolutionary timetable, over decades. I journey all over the world and enjoy local delicacies as part of my travel-writing vocation. How could I renounce octopus, whether served in Greece, Japan, or the Caribbean, where octopus is considered a local delicacy? A friend recently told me about being served "a baby octopus" on her plate while visiting Japan. "So delicious," she sighed. I wept at this story.

The foundations of my evolutionary change occurred in the fall of 1994, when my then ten-year-old daughter informed me matter-of-factly that she was a vegetarian. *Why*, I asked? "I don't want to eat anything that has a face." While I was a bit miffed that I'd have to cook a separate menu for her, my daughter's announcement set my brain whirring. Should I, too, be feeling bad for eating be-faced creatures? Was my daughter morally superior to me? Would I have to learn how to cook tofu? How would I supply her with protein?

Mainstream culinary culture has taken a quarter century to catch up with my daughter. In 2000, Harvard Law School acceded to student demand and established an animal law course. Many law schools across the United States followed suit. In 2002, Germany amended its constitution to raise the protection of nonhuman animals to a fundamental level.

Over the past several years, I've become profoundly grateful that humans—myself included—have become enlightened about the consciousness and feeling of all creatures. On July 7, 2012, the Cambridge Declaration on Consciousness announced a universal proclamation on animal sentience. This group of cognitive and computational neuroscientists had assembled to proclaim that nonhuman animals, including the great apes, dolphins, elephants, birds, and octopuses, possess pathways throughout their brains that show emotional feelings. Just because an animal doesn't have a neocortex like a human, doesn't mean it can't feel. Octopuses have "neurological substrates" shared by *Homo sapiens* that generate consciousness in spite of the fact that the two species diverged on the tree of life about six hundred million years ago. And look very different to the outside world.

While I fully supported these strides in animal welfare and seriously cut down on my meat consumption, I wasn't ready to give up on *all meats*. More significantly, I knew there were still some gastronomies I had yet to encounter.

On my first Greek voyage to the southern Peloponnesus in 2007, I discovered the gastronomic delights of the octopus. Each day at sunrise, I sat in tranquil meditation, gazing over the morning catch of octopuses drying out on the glass lampposts. Their voluptuous forms adorned every streetlamp up and down the embarcadero. A salt-fish smell wafted up into the street cafes from the peaceful blue-green waves lapping over the seawall.

Nearing noon every day, the charcoal fires flickered in front of the tavernas lining the *paraliakó diádromo*. Smoke swirled upward from the burning coals, enticing the passersby. I was no exception. Previously, I'd despised octopus dishes with a vengeance because of the rubbery consistency that's ubiquitous in the United States. But in Greece, I experienced an epicurean heaven of soft textured, melt-in-the-mouth, succulent, juicy rings. Each had been cooked to a precise point of perfection.

In Neapoli, Hellenic cooks expertly chopped the mollusks into exacting sections, roasted these morsels with a drizzle of olive oil and a dash of salt. I ate at the same taverna each day with friends, with the same menu: ouzo and charcoal-broiled octopus.

At the time, I unwittingly endorsed Aristotle's twenty-four-century-old opinion: "The octopus is a stupid creature … for it will approach a man's hand if it be lowered in the water." But thankfully, human knowledge has evolved since the time of Aristotle. We now know empirically that the octopus is not the least bit stupid. With three hearts and nine brains, studies of octopus' acumen continue to reveal new insights into this species. And as my YouTube deep-dive confirmed, when an octopus explores an extended hand, it's showing curiosity and courage. The octopus does not shrink from learning what the hand represents.

Over the past several years, I've become profoundly grateful that humans—myself included—are growing enlightened about the consciousness and feelings of all creatures. In addition to the Cambridge Declaration on Consciousness on animal sentience, we've learned that while the octopus genome isn't quite as large as a human's, it contains a greater number of protein-coding genes—about 33,000, compared to less than 25,000 of these genes in *Homo sapiens*. This abundance of protein-coding genes allows octopuses to respond quickly to their environment with an aptitude that humans don't possess. As Stephen Hawking has said about humans, "We are just an advanced breed of monkeys on a minor planet of a very average star. But we can understand the Universe. That makes us something very special." Special enough to treat our fellow creatures with consideration and compassion. The more I learned about octopuses made me vow never to eat them again.

In *Animal Rights: What Everyone Needs to Know*, Paul Waldau chronicles the timeline for human-animal interactions spanning thirty-five thousand years. From the 20,000-year-old cave drawings at Lascaux, France, to the Treaties of Amsterdam and Rome in the late 1990s that set up laws defining nonhuman animals as "sentient beings,"humans have acknowledged the importance of animals, and their rights have gained credence.

During my latest visit to Greece, in 2019, I carried within me a new understanding of this sea creature's consciousness. I prayed that these beings didn't have an existential memory of me devouring dozens of their kin on the Neapoli shores and hoped they understood how boldly I now celebrated their intelligence.

On this recent trip, the day before a hosted luncheon at the acclaimed Imerovigli Restaurant in Piraeus—renowned for its octopus and squid—I made a pilgrimage to the Temple of Apollo at Delphi. Hoping to breathe in the methane and carbon dioxide vapors that scientists now think allowed female oracles to predict the future for ancient Greeks, I meditated on the weighty Greek aphorism, "Know thyself." Inscribed on the *pronaos* of Apollo's Temple, this maxim has been ascribed to playwright Aeschylus in *Prometheus Bound*, to Socrates as he wrote his history *Memorabilia*, and to Plato, who used his characterization of Socrates for this motivational axiom. Whether it was the ninety-five-degree temperatures in the direct sun of high noon that day at Delphi or the methane miasma seeping up around me, I reaffirmed my resolve. I had to honor my new understanding about and compassion for the octopus.

On the next day of my enlightenment, I decided not to dine on the creatures. At the luncheon at the Hymerovigli, the memories of the potent flavors and softness of texture from thirteen years prior didn't even tempt me to taste the fragrant grilled slices. In spite of my slight embarrassment at refusing the host's offerings, I stood strong. As we sat in the open air above Piraeus harbor, yachts and sailboats bobbing in the noon sun sparkling off the bluest water, I was at peace with my decision.

As a garrulous member of our party repeated an outlandish tale about a breakfast smoothie for the third time, all eyes and ears were focused on this lighthearted anecdote. At the other end of the table, I meditated on the serving plate in sadness. The magnificent beings I held in my hands were already dead, and by this logic, there might be no harm in my partaking of the charbroiled meat. But the immobile cuttlefish still looked like cuttlefish, and the squid tentacles splayed about on the plate still seemed to move. Both were cephalopods with neurological substrates of emotions and feeling shared with the octopus. I passed the bier on.

Amid the din of lunchtime laughter and conversation, no one noticed that, at one point, I held the separate platter of grilled octopus in my hands for several minutes. Then a whisper touched an ear.

Know thyself.

As if the Delphic oracle stood nearby.

Know thyself. And know all other creatures.

Socrates' ghost gusted past my other ear. I was taken aback momentarily.

Their spirits do reside in Greece, I reasoned. The octopus' sarcophagus weighed heavy in my hands.

In his philosophies, Socrates always emphasized action over words, and all at once I was seized by a fervent notion. I could run to the high-walled street's edge and upend the plate into the harbor—a burial at sea for these creatures lying prone in my hands.

Instead, I followed my next impulse: I quietly set the oval platter on the edge of the table and gently covered it with the white cloth napkin. The pall had been placed. I entreated past and future Greek gods for the octopuses' peaceful passage into Poseidon's realm. I thoroughly enjoyed my delightful Greek salad.

Loggerhead turtle hatchling

Turtle Tracks

Barbara J. Euser

The loggerhead turtle swam slowly toward the shore. Moonlight reflected on the surface of the sea, so brightly it outshone the stars. As the turtle reached the sand, she used her paddle arms to push her way onto the beach. Her paddle legs pushed against the sand. With great effort, she climbed across the hard, wet sand until she reached the softer, dry sand. She kept going. How far would the water rise with the tide? How far up would waves splash when pushed by a south wind? She climbed further, until she decided her eggs would be safe. Then she started to dig. With her paddle arms, she moved kilos and kilos of sand. When her nest hole was about a meter deep, she positioned herself so her eggs would drop into the deepest part of the hole. Finally, she was able to relax and deposit almost one hundred eggs. When she finished, she had to get to work again. She covered the eggs with the sand she had scraped from the hole. When she finished, there was still a slight depression in the sand. She headed back to the sea, creating a new track. As she pushed one paddle arm, then the other, then each paddle leg, through the sand, the sky lightened. Soon it would be dawn.

I begin my beach walk at about nine a.m. I would have liked to start earlier, before the sun hit the sand, but at least I had made it. Twice a week I walk here, from the ferry terminal for the island of Elafonisos to Mangano Beach Bar. I am looking for sea turtle tracks, which indicate a new loggerhead turtle nest. From May through August, loggerhead turtles, *Caretta caretta*, return to the beaches all around Vatika Bay and the Myrtoon Sea to lay their eggs. Once every three or four years, a mother turtle will return to the place where she herself was born.

For the past five years, as a volunteer for the local non-governmental organization Toulipa Goulymi, I have walked this same stretch of beach, searching for turtle tracks. Toulipa Goulymi has been recording the turtle nests along the beaches—and the hatchlings—since 2014.

As the number of volunteers increased, and volunteers regularly walked more beaches, more and more nests have been identified. All together, we identified over 200 turtle nests on local beaches in 2018. ARCHELON, the sea turtle protection organization of Greece, has added Vatika Bay to its map of documented loggerhead nesting sites in Greece.

ARCHELON trained two leaders of Toulipa Goulymi, Yiannis and Maria, to open the nests and confirm that they held eggs. A mother turtle may prepare a nest and be unable to lay eggs in it. She covers it as though it is full, returns to the sea, and may return the next night and build another nest. Yiannis and Maria try to open each nest that has been reported.

As a volunteer, I have participated in opening a nest—but only to the point of digging out the heaviest part of the sand and taking measurements. We start by deciding where the eggs are most likely to be. Then we use our hands, just as the mother turtle used her flippers, digging up kilos and kilos of sand until our arms ache. As soon as we see the tops of the translucent, ping pong ball-sized eggs, Yiannis and Maria take over, gently dusting the sand from the fragile eggs. We note the nest's geographical location, its latitude and longitude, its width and depth, and distance from the sea. In exceptional cases, when the nest is too close to the sea, and risks being inundated, Yiannis and Maria dig a new nest farther from the sea, and move the eggs to a safe location. Once all the measurements have been recorded, we push all the sand back over the eggs. We position a wide-meshed metal screen over the nest to protect the eggs from digging dogs, foxes and other predators. Then we build a fence of sticks, or place a metal cage over the nest, along with a printed notice that this is the nest of the endangered species of sea turtle *Caretta caretta*, and thus protected under European law.

About two months later, volunteers begin monitoring the turtle hatch. But the hatching may not start until after ten at night—or even later—and not be complete for hours. Who can do this work night after night during hatching season? Very few. I have only watched one night-time hatch. The nest was on the beach right in front of the largest hotel in Neapolis. After eating dinner in town, I received a text message from Maria, telling me where to go. She and several grade-school students were already there monitoring the situation. I knelt down in the sand and joined them.

The two-inch-long hatchlings were just digging their way up through the sand. They pushed and scrambled against each other to reach air to breathe. Then they began their perilous journey to the sea. Our job that night was to create a corridor for the hatchlings and make sure they reached the sea. Using strips of fabric attached to bamboo stakes, we marked the edges of the hatchlings' path to the sea. It is essential that each hatchling makes the journey on its own: it must imprint the way to the sea in its brain, so it can return to the same location when it is fully mature.

Of the approximately one hundred eggs the mother turtle laid, about eighty will hatch. Of those eighty, only half—about forty—will make it to the water. They are born knowing that they must seek the moonlight reflecting on the surface of the sea. Thus, turtle hatchlings automatically head toward the brightest light. Along undeveloped beaches, like the one I walk from Pounta to Mangano, there are no competing sources of light. However, turtles hatching on the beaches of the town of Neapolis, or near the road in Limnes, are easily confused. Lights from the restaurants and hotels outshine the moon. Streetlights are full moons in fatal disguise.

Having finally made it to the sea, the hatchling turtles are the object of many predators. For protection, they may hide in Sargasso weed or other floating plants or debris. Within a few years, only a fraction of the forty turtles that made it to the sea are still alive. The odds of survival are so poor that only one in a thousand eggs will live to become a mature turtle able to reproduce. Out of ten nests of one hundred eggs each, only one turtle will actually return to the beach where it was born.

I recall these odds of survival every time I walk this beach. I carry a large plastic trash bag with me. The primary purpose of my walk is to look for fresh turtle tracks, but the secondary reason is to pick up trash that accumulates here. Some of the trash is heedlessly dropped by visitors to the beach: plastic cups, plastic straws, plastic bags, plastic mesh, cigarette lighters, butts and filters. Other trash is washed in from the sea: lengths of cord, fishing line, smoke flares, plastic glow sticks, and tiny—and tinier—pieces of plastic. All of these pieces of trash are potential turtle killers. The dead turtle found most recently on the beach was strangled by a plastic bag. Not long ago, another dead turtle was found with no marks of violence. Perhaps, weighted down by the many pieces of indigestible plastic it had eaten, it was unable to come to the surface to breathe, and drowned.

In the past three years, seventy-six dead turtles have been found on the beaches of Vatika Bay and the Myrtoon Sea. These dead turtles represent seven hundred and sixty turtle nests, seventy-six thousand turtle eggs. Most of the dead turtles bear signs of deliberate aggression, most often smashed heads. Others have carapaces cut to pieces by propellers. Who is responsible for killing these rare, endangered creatures? The knee-jerk response is "Fishermen." Turtles may become entangled in fishing nets, damaging the nets and potentially eating the catch. Greek fishermen have yet to adopt fishing nets with turtle-excluder devices. Sea turtles may be viewed by fishermen as competitors for the limited source of the fishermen's livelihood. Some turtles may be killed out of pure malice.

How can local attitudes toward sea turtles be changed? Education —awareness raising—is the answer. So Yiannis visits several school classrooms each year with a slide show presentation. Elementary school students from Monemvasia have painted signs which were posted on beaches where turtles nest. Toulipa Goulymi organizes beach clean-up walks, and parents bring their children. Other volunteers like me walk the beaches wearing our T-shirts from ARCHELON or Toulipa Goulymi, so that everyone who sees us is reminded once again that turtles must be protected. At the first Pavlopetri Eco-Marine Film Festival held in July 2019, two films dealt with sea turtles: one a winner of the International Ocean Film Festival's 2019 Student Film Competition entitled *Turtle Crisis*, the other a full-length documentary entitled *A Plastic Ocean*. After the screening of *A Plastic Ocean*, two teachers approached one of the Festival organizers. They said they wanted every school child in Neapolis to see that film.

Local attitudes toward sea turtles lag behind international recognition: In April 2017, Mission Blue, the prestigious international marine protection organization, designated Vatika Bay and the Myrtoon Sea as the first Hope Spot in Greece. Mission Blue made its designation based on the iconic species that inhabit Vatika Bay—whales, dolphins, monk seals and loggerhead turtles—in proximity to the submerged archeological site of Pavlopetri.

From where I am, about four kilometers from the ferry terminal and Pavlopetri, I can see Mangano Beach Bar half a kilometer ahead. And I see the distinctive tracks of a turtle etched in the wet sand. Last night, a mother turtle was here! Her tail has left a mark like a knife, cutting a trail. As I get closer, I can see the scoops of sand taken by each of her paddle arms and legs. The tracks head upwards into the sand dunes. I am amazed she travelled so far uphill. I see the depression in the sand where she has dug her nest and then covered it. And I see where she headed back to the sea, leaving a parallel set of tracks. The incoming tide is already washing away the tracks in the hard sand. In a few hours, the wind will blow loose sand into the tracks, leaving them indistinguishable from other irregularities. For thousands of years, this camouflage worked in favor of the turtle hatchlings, rendering the nest nearly invisible. Today, with threats from humans on the rise, the sea turtles can use all the help we can give. I take photos of the tracks and nest area and send them to Maria. Then I gather some sticks and mark the nest so Yiannis and Maria can come and open it. I am bursting with this news. I want to celebrate this small victory.

I continue my walk, picking up pieces of plastic trash, and I look out at the Bay. Somewhere out there, there is a small head breaking the surface of the water, taking a deep breath, and diving down, slowly swimming into the open sea.

Approaching the island of Hydra

Author Biographies

Daphne Beyers grew up near Amish country in northeastern Pennsylvania, often finding herself caught in traffic behind wheel and buggy carriages. She's lived many places including London, New York City, San Francisco, Berkeley, and Palm Springs. Daphne taught herself to program at the age of thirteen and works as a computer consultant for various Fortune 500 companies. Her essay, "Existential Cafe," was published in an award-winning anthology of Parisian stories, *Wandering in Paris: Luminaries and Love in the City of Light.*

Sandra Bracken made the first of many journeys alone to Peru where she walked the hills around Sacsayhuaman, photographed the stone-work there and chartered a plane to fly over the lines at Nazca—all in the pursuit of art. She has a Master's Degree in Fine Arts, taught drawing for twenty years and has exhibited sculpture and drawings in galleries and museums in the U.S. She collaborated on a collection of poems and collages, *Meet Me at the Wayside Body Shop*, and pro-duced a chapbook of poems, *New Moon.*

Her travel stories were included in *Venturing in Ireland: Quest for the Modern Celtic Soul; Venturing in Italy: Puglia, Land between Two Seas; Wandering in Paris: Luminaries and Love in the City of Light; Wandering in Cornwall: Mystery, Mirth and Transformation in the Land of Ancient Celts* and *Wandering in Andalusia: The Soul of Southern Spain.* She lives in Maryland near her three children and five grandchildren. Her most recent travels have been with her husband—in pursuit of fish.

Connie Burke left San Francisco, California in 1979. She set out for her Ithaka, hoping to make her journey a long one, full of adventure, full of discovery. Settling in Athens, Greece, she taught English literature at the American College of Greece and the University of Maryland, European Division, Athens. Leaving academia, she co-founded Writers' Workshops International and published popular travel literature with Travelers' Tales, an imprint of Solas house. She is the co-editor of the travel series; *Venturing in Southern Greece: the Vatika Odysseys, Venturing in Ireland: Quest for the Modern Celtic Soul and Venturing in Italy: Puglia, Land between Two Seas.* Today she walks along the ancient stoned streets of Athens and reflects upon the wisdom of Socrates, realizing how little she still understands about life, about ourselves and about this enigmatic world around us.

Barbara J. Euser writes about nature, gardening and travel. She is a retired lawyer and Foreign Service Officer. Currently she devotes much of her time to working on projects with non-profit organizations, including the International Community Development Foundation, Nicaragua-Projekt, the Greek chapter of the Alliance for the Restoration of Cultural Heritage, and the Greek environmental NGO Toulipa Goulymi. She lives in the southern Peloponnese. She spends her free time sailing, gardening and tending her olive farm.

Annelize Goedbloed was born in Celebes, Indonesia—a Dutch colony at the time—and spent her toddler years as a "guest" of the emperor of Japan. After the war she and her parents (both physicians) were evacuated to Holland. Early exposure to creeping and crawling animal life inspired her to study parasitology and marine biology. While birthing her four children, she needed to be at home and thus started breeding Texel sheep and special chicken breeds. She served several years as a member of the board of pedigree sheep breeders of South Holland. With her son, Annelize started a company (BioClin) that now proudly holds a patent on a plant-derived polysaccharide with anti-infection properties. She has written clinical trial reports and lectures in English worldwide on scientific findings. With thirteen grandchildren, the family breeding ventures are obviously continuing.

Thomas Harrell has joined the ranks of former lawyers who became writers. After sixteen years working for a Wall Street firm, the last six on dialysis, he received a new kidney eight years ago. With this second chance, he decided to leave the law and pursue two of his life passions: travel and writing. He has traveled to numerous countries, although not nearly enough yet. He has written about travel in several of these countries, including Argentina, Bosnia, China and Italy. A frequent contributor to the Wanderland anthology series, Tom also writes personal essays, many set in the South, where he was raised. He studied history and politics in college and is writing a spy novel set during the Civil War. He lives in San Francisco, California.

Donna Hemmila finds the best travel experiences arise from her inability to understand maps, even the electronic kind that talks to you. She inevitably turns left down narrow passageways when she should have gone straight. At those times, she thinks of her grandmother, Sophie, who left Poland at the age of twenty-two, bound for America with nine dollars in her pocket and a desire only to see what was waiting around the next bend. Hint: It will always be something amazing you didn't expect. Donna has worked as a news reporter, business editor, and speechwriter and was a contributor to *Wandering in Andalusia: The Soul of Southern Spain*. She lives in Berkeley, California, and writes children's books.

Laurie McAndish King writes about 20-foot-long Australian earthworms, being rescued from a kidnapper in Tunisia, and an Ivy League astrophysicist's explanation of how flying saucers are powered. Her award-winning true stories and photography have appeared in *Smithsonian* magazine, the *San Francisco Chronicle*, *The Best Women's Travel Writing*, and other magazines and literary anthologies. Laurie's most recent book, *Your Crocodile has Arrived: More True Stories from a Curious Traveler*, was called "thoroughly engrossing" by the Midwest Book Review and earned a first-place Independent Press Award. A story in her first book, *Lost, Kidnapped, Eaten Alive*, won the coveted Lowell Thomas Gold Award. Laurie also wrote *An Erotic Alphabet* (for which she was dubbed "The Shel Silverstein of Erotica").

Gayle McGill grew up in St. Catharines Ontario, with four brothers in a poor but high-spirited family. She came of age in the sixties and spent her young adult years carting an enormous backpack around the globe. Her love of travel has not diminished. She has been identified as a tree hugger, music lover, science wonderer and one who worries way too much about feminist issues. Her work career has been long and varied— teacher, barmaid, travel agent, and for the last three decades programmer. Gayle has written thousands of lines of code that live on in software systems all over the Bay Area. Her code has won acclaim and has been translated into many languages. She is also the author two Solas award-winning stories published in the Wanderland Writers anthology, *Wandering in Andalusia,* a novel set in the Australian Outback, a guide to the best conifer hikes in California and many technical "How To" manuals. Oakland has been her home for the past thirty years where she lives with her belligerent garden, amicable husband John and daughter Anna nearby.

Mary Jean (MJ) Pramik, a coalminer's daughter and great granddaughter of the Mongolian plain, has survived the COVID-19 Pandemic without howling. After all, San Francisco, the Manhattan of the West, lives a rather cultured life without symphony, opera, and other concerts. As a trained molecular biologist and vaccine researcher, MJ has enjoyed viral attack experience. She knew it was heading to the planet. Prepandemic, she has published copiously in medical journals and mainstream publications such as *Good Housekeeping* and the *National Enquirer.* MJ's contributed to the Travelers' Tales *"Venturing in"* travel series on the Canal du Midi, Southern Greece, Southern Ireland, and Wanderland Writers anthologies on Costa Rica, Bali, Cornwall, England, Andalusia, Spain, and Cuba. She has won several Solas Travel Writing awards for her travel essays. MJ blogs about travel and science at *Dear Earth: Travel in Times of Catastrophic Change.* She is a member of the Community of Writers of the High Sierra, the Association of

Writers and Writing Programs, and the American Academy of Poets. She has completed her first novel, *GEM of Egypt*, and a collection of poetry. Her poem, "Rocks, Stones," was nominated for a Pushcart Prize.

Anne Sigmon washed out of high school and college PE. After college, she headed for San Francisco and a communications career. Exotic travel was the stuff of dreams until, at 38, she married Jack, took tea with erstwhile headhunters in Borneo and climbed Mt. Kilimanjaro at 43. Five years later, she was zapped by a career-ending stroke caused by an obscure autoimmune disease called Antiphospholipid Syndrome (APS). She may be stuck with blood thinners and a damaged brain, but she's still traveling to the wild from Botswana to Syria, Iran and Uzbekistan.

Anne's essays and award-winning travel stories have appeared in national publications including *Good Housekeeping* and *Stroke Connection* magazines and the American Heart Association website. Her work has appeared in the Best Travel Writing.com, Wanderlust and Lipstick and GeoEx.com digital magazines, and in a dozen anthologies, most recently Bradt Guide's *To Oldly Go* and *The Best Women's Travel Writing*, Vol. 12. She is currently working on a memoir about her experience with stroke and autoimmune disease. Anne lives in Lafayette, California, with her husband, Jack Martin.

EDITOR BIOGRAPHIES

Joanna Biggar is a teacher, writer and traveler whose special places of the heart include the California coast and the South of France. As a professional writer for thirty years, she has written poetry, fiction, personal essays, features, news and travel articles for hundreds of publications including The Washington Post Magazine, Psychology Today, The International Herald Tribune, and The Wall Street Journal. Her most recent travel essays have appeared in the Wandering series, whose anthologies include books on Costa Rica, Bali, Paris, Cornwall, Andalusia and Cuba. *That Paris Year*, the first in a trilogy of novels, was published by Alan Squire Publishing in 2010, followed by *Melanie's Song* in 2019. She has taught journalism, creative writing, personal essay and travel writing in many venues, and has juried the annual awards for the Northern California chapter of the Society of Professional Journalists. She serves on the Board of Directors of Emiliano Zapata Street Academy in Oakland, California, where she makes her home, and is a longtime member of the Society of Woman Geographers.

Linda Watanabe McFerrin (www.lwmcferrin.com) is a poet, travel writer, novelist and contributor to numerous newspapers, magazines and anthologies. She is the author of two poetry collections, past editor of a popular Northern California guidebook and a winner of the Katherine Anne Porter Prize for Fiction. Her award-winning book-length fiction titles include *Namako: Sea Cucumber, The Hand of Buddha* and *Dead Love* (Stone Bridge Press, 2009), a Bram Stoker Award Finalist for Superior Achievement in a Novel.

In addition, Linda has co-edited twelve anthologies, including the *Hot Flashes: sexy little stories & poems series*; judged the San Francisco Literary Awards, the Josephine Miles Award for Literary Excellence and the Kiriyama Prize; served as a visiting mentor for the Loft Mentor Series; and been guest faculty at the Oklahoma Arts Institute. A past NEA Panelist and juror for the Marin Literary Arts Council and the founder of Left Coast Writers®, she has led workshops in Greece, France, Italy, England, Ireland, Central America, Indonesia, Scotland, Spain and the United States and has mentored a long list of accomplished writers and best-selling authors toward publication. Her most recent book, *Navigating the Divide* (Alan Squire Publishing, 2019) was a Next Generation Indie Book Awards Finalist.

www.ingramcontent.com/pod-product-compliance
Lightning Source LLC
Chambersburg PA
CBHW060321030426
42336CB00011B/1154